DECIPHERING LEGALESE

A PRACTICAL HANDBOOK FOR LAW STUDENTS

Gitanjali Thapar

BlueRose ONE.com
Stories Matter
NewDelhi • London

BLUEROSE PUBLISHERS
India | U.K.

BlueRose ONE
Stories Matter
New Delhi • London

For permissions requests or inquiries regarding this publication, please contact:

BLUEROSE PUBLISHERS
www.BlueRoseONE.com
info@bluerosepublishers.com
+91 8882 898 898
+4407342408967

ISBN: 978-93-7018-570-8

Cover design: Aafiya Saifi
Typesetting: Manisha Rawat

First Edition: January 2026

Preface

Law and language are fundamentally intertwined. Laws are expressed through language and legal language provides a framework for the articulation of rights and obligations. Moreover law, mediated by language is an important tool for social control and maintaining social welfare. It is through Language that rights are defined, duties are specified, onuses are generated, and justice is delivered. In the contemporary power dynamics, command over legalese, can influence legal outcomes and shape public opinions. *Deciphering Legal Language: A Practical Handbook for Law Students* presents a concise and insightful guide to understand and use legal language with precision and purpose.

The handbook is student oriented and envisions that the complexity and elusiveness allied with the legal language can be deconstructed. By blending practical examples with clear elucidations, an effort has been made to decipher the legal terminology, structure, and reasoning that shapes legal communication. The book can be added to the reading corpus as a valuable resource for anyone seeking to read, draft, or interpret legal texts with greater resilience and jauntiness. I am delighted to introduce this work, which foresees to refine the reader's skills and deepens appreciation for the power of language at the heart of the law.

Gitanjali

Foreword

Legal literacy stands as a cornerstone of an informed and just society. In a world increasingly governed by laws, understanding the language that articulates them becomes not only an academic pursuit but a civic necessity. Law and language exist in a symbiotic relationship, each shaping and reinforcing the other. Through language, laws are created, interpreted, and applied; through law, language finds its most precise and consequential expression. This book, *Deciphering Legal Language: A Practical Handbook for Law Students,* underscores the significance of mastering this interplay, guiding readers toward greater clarity and confidence while crossing the legal sphere. What sets this handbook apart is its pragmatic orientation.

Truly speaking, Legal language often intimidates with its complexity, archaic expressions, and nuanced constructions. The author, with commendable sensitivity to the student's perspective, deconstructs these challenges through lucid explanations and relatable examples. By bridging theoretical understanding with practical application, the book demystifies legal terminology and reasoning, offering students a structured pathway to interpret and produce legal texts effectively. It not only sharpens linguistic competence but also cultivates analytical precision, which lies at the core of legal education and practice. This work arrives as a timely contribution to the evolving discipline of legal studies, where communication forms the bridge between knowledge and justice. Its insights will benefit not only aspiring lawyers but also scholars, educators, and all those invested in understanding the intricate fabric of legal expression. By engaging with this handbook, readers will refine their interpretative skills, strengthen their command over legal discourse, and gain a deeper appreciation for the language that upholds the boundaries of rights, duties, and justice.

I extend my heartfelt congratulations to Dr. Gitanjali on the publication of this valuable work. Her dedication, clarity of thought, and commitment to legal scholarship shine through every page of this book. May this book reach all those who seek knowledge and may Dr. Gitanjali continue to illuminate the path of learning with wisdom, integrity, and purpose.

With a lot of Blessings.

Professor (Dr.) Sanjay Sindhu

Chairman, Legal Advisory Monitoring Committee, H P University

Advisor, Shoolini University of Management and Biotechnology, Distt Solan, H P

Former Dean, Faculty of Law,

Former Chairman, Department of Laws,

Former Director, UILS, Ava Lodge Campus,

Himachal Pradesh University,

Summerhill, Shimla 171005 H.P. (INDIA)

Contents

Chapter-1
The Linguistic Characteristics of Legal Language

Legal Language has a significant role to play in the Legal Profession. For the Lawmen in India English Language has essentially gained prominence as the Lingua Franca. The language used in the legal discourse worldwide is English. However, the language used in the legal field is distinct from the usual general English. Hence, legal language needs to be approached as English for Specific Purposes. The term ESP refers to the use of language which focuses on a particular communicative needs and practices of particular social groups. ESP is defined to meet the specific requirements of the user in different fields of study and professions. According to the domain of use in various field of discourse, ESP regulates the grammatical and lexical style in a specific way. Being India's integrating language, English as a language has a unique distinction. Legal Language acquires a very prominent place as the language of law. Legalese or the Legal Language is made up of its own distinct characteristics and features. It is illustrated in the court rooms during cross-examination, in drafting, pleading a case or in the court craft. The jargon vocabulary used in the court of law lends a distinctive quality to the legal language. Legal Language has acquired a special place as ESP. English for Specific Purposes has its own domain and scope. In the present era of globalization, privatization and liberalization it has become imperative to possess the knowledge of rights and duties, rules and regulations and the law of the land *jus soli.* Glanville Williams points out that language is perhaps the greatest of all human inventions and also the chief medium of thoughts. For Lawyers language has a special role as it is the greatest instrument of social control. Law controls and governs the society through verbal maneuver of rights, duties wrong etc. English is a global language and has been credited as the official language of the courts in India and also in the international arena .In the past few decades English as a language has also acquired significant importance as the language of international law. In Indian perspective English is the core language of law and has been established as the bridge Language connecting people with the State.

The pragmatic importance of the legal language can be adjudged by the inclusion of numerous Greek, Latin and Roman terms and maxims. Legal Language is rich in content and style and its intricacies are drawn from the rich corpus of legal history and jurisprudential content. Latin expressions abound in law, phrases like *ab initio, bona fide, mala fide, prima facie* are also a part of jargon vocabulary. Law is the most jargon-ridden language amongst the specialist language, an interesting example of it is "as to", as to the question, counsel has no reply. Legal terms *like plaintiff, defendant, amicus curiae, caveat emptor, status quo, suo motu , sine qua* non are few examples of words incorporated in the legal terminology. Maxims which are found upon justice and good sense acts as a guide for the administration of justice. Legal Maxims are established truths which convey eternal facts involved in the interpretation and execution of law. Maxims like: *Actus Non Facti Reum Nisi Mens Sit Rea* (Latin), *Audi Alteram Partem*, *Ignorantia Facti Excusat Ignorantia Juris Non Excusat , Res Ipsa Loquitor* are an integral part of legalese, used for communication and discourses in the court of Law. Maxims are the life blood of law and are understood by every person of the legal fraternity.

Human beings have mastered cognitive language communication. The use of language is crucial to any legal system. The lawmakers characteristically use language to draft laws. Till a bill is tabled before the parliament number of speculative thoughts and developments are involved. When a bill becomes a law it largely depends upon the draftsman to incorporate effective legal terminology so as to enhance its legal accessibility to the common man.

The Language of the Law is a type of register and it acts as a reference guide for a variety of language appropriate to different occasions and situations of use. Tiersman suggests:

"Legal Language has been called an argot, a dialect, a register, a style and even a separate language. In fact, it is best described with the relatively new term sublanguage, a sublanguage that has its own specialized grammar, a limited subject matter, contains lexical, syntactical and semantic restrictions …legal language is a complex collection of linguistic habits that have developed over many centuries and that jurists have learned to use quite strategically." (Tiersman, 1999)

The language of the law is very distinctive and its lexical and syntactical patterns lends it a special characteristic of English used for Specific purpose in the Legal domain. The nature and function of law has a global significance and makes the use of English as a globally understood legal Language. The legal language has developed particular linguistic features like: lexical, syntactical and pragmatic to fulfil the demands and contemporary needs of the law in the present times. The linguistic characteristics of the language of the law have profound implications for legal interpretation, execution, enactment and also translation.

Legal language has extraordinary linguistic features which can be identified across different legal languages which are visibly manifested with respect to lexicon, syntax, pragmatics and style. Legal lexicon is full of archaic words with formal and ritualistic usage. The word sequences along with the usage of common words with uncommon meanings and words of over-precision is an important component of Legal Language.

The language of Law is highly formal and impersonal written in an effective style joined with considerable intricacy, complexity and an operative dimension. Complex sentence structures with the use of passive voice, multiple disavowals and prepositional phrases are widely used in legal language. Another pragmatic consideration in legal texts is ambiguity, vagueness and other uncertainties found mainly in the bare acts, statutes and contracts. Legal writing is also characterized by an impersonal style, with the extensive use of declarative sentences pronouncing rights, rule of law and obligations.

Legal terminology is very different from everyday vocabulary and is generally archaic. In English, there is abundant number of terms originating from Latin. The prominent feature of legal style is very long sentences. This tendency for lengthy sentences is due to the need to place all information on a particular topic in one complete unit in order to reduce the ambiguity that may arise if the conditions of a provision are placed in separate sentences. The law is always phrased in an impersonal manner so as to address several audiences at once. For example a lawyer typically starts with *"May it Please the Court"* addressing the judge or judges in the third person. Old and Middle English archaic expressions like, "The petitioner has to respectfully showeth" reflects at the inherent archaic use of words.

Lawyers try to be as precise as possible and use general, vague and flexible language. As Tiersma notes, "flexible and abstract language is typical of constitutions which are ideally written to endure over time" (1999, p.176). Historical factors and stylistic tradition explain the character of present-day Legal English.Many old phrases and words can be traced back to Anglo-Saxon, old French, and Medieval Latin. Legal language has many common terms with uncommon meanings. According to Danet, "legal language has an inclination for using familiar words (but) with uncommon meanings" (2005, p.59). For example, the word 'assignment' which is generally known as something assigned - a task or a duty. Similarly the words like 'contract', 'valid', 'discretion' have an altogether different meaning. Students of translation have learnt the word in its general literal meaning and they continue to know it as such until they have to translate an assignment, which is a legal document.

Therefore, one of the tasks for the legal translator is to identify the legal meaning and distinguish it from its ordinary meaning before rendering it appropriately into target language. For instance, in translating English contracts or documents related to contract law, legal terms frequently encountered include offer, consideration, performance, remedy and assignment. These words in English have an ordinary meaning used in non-legal settings. They are also legal technical terms that carry special legal significance in contract law. In English contract law, 'offer' refers to a promise which when accepted constitutes an agreement; 'Consideration' refers to the price paid, not thought or thinking in ordinary usage; 'Performance' specifically refers to the doing of that which is required by a contract or condition. A contract is discharged by performance. The expression specific performance in contract law is not literally what it says. It actually means where damages would be inadequate compensation for the breach of an agreement, the contracting parties may be compelled to perform what was agreed to be done by a decree of specific performance, e.g. the sale, purchase or lease of land, or recovery of unique chattels. The word remedy is not just a way of solving a problem but a legal means whereby breach of a right is prevented or redress is given, e.g. damages and/or injunction. 'Assignment' in contract law means transfer of property or right. The legal translator when trying to identify and ascertain the meaning of a particular word with both ordinary and legal meanings or a word with several legal meanings, one can make use of the context in which the word occurs and interpret accordingly. Thus, Rhetoric is synonym in Legal Language, clearly visible in the court judgement e.g., one is not with the truth "but the truth the whole truth and nothing but the truth".

Chapter-2
Legal Syntax

Syntax refers to the "the arrangement of words and phrases to create well-formed sentences in a language". The legal Syntax is unique in its own ways. It is too complicated to be understood easily by laypersons and is marked by long and complex sentences, too many embedded clauses, and overuse of certain classes to words. The legal language comprises of a very large number of long compound and complex sentences. The compound sentences are full of many main clauses and they also make the sentences very long. The complex sentences are usually full of various subordinate clauses which are independent and finally dependent on the main clause(s) for the meaning to be discovered. Bentham has noted that lawyers have favoured "long windedness" and suggested that "the shorter the sentence the better".(Jenny Bentham 264)Too many modifications, over-caution, embedded clauses, atypical word order and insertion of words or phrases where they are not usually used in the usual discourse cause complexity of sentences.

The Preamble of Indian Constitution is a unique and strong example of solemn and stately legal language. Though the sentence contains 84 words, it is systematically and logically divided into different parts and each part is like a poetic line with the initial capital letter of the word. It is all inclusive and encompasses the mission and vision of the country. Certain words are foregrounding by highlighting them in bold font. It demonstrates how sentence structure, grammatical precision and word order coveys the legal intent, hierarchy of values and expresses authority.

The syntax of the preamble to the Indian constitution is carefully crafted to convey authority, clarity and constitutionality. It is written in a single, long, coherent sentence which is structured using participle phrases, like "having solemnly resolved" and infinitive phrases like "to constitute India into …" to reflect upon purpose and action. The use of parallelism in phrases like "Justice, social, economic and political" and "Liberty of thought, expression, belief, faith and worship" lays emphasis on each ideal.

"WE, THE PEOPLE OF INDIA, having solemnly resolved to constitute

India into a **SOVEREIGN, SOCIALIST, SECULAR, DEMOCRATIC**,

REPUBLIC and to secure all its citizens:

JUSTICE, social, economic and political;

LIBERTY of thought, expression, belief, faith and worship;

EQUALITY of status and of opportunity; and to promote among them all

FRATERNITY assuring the dignity of the individual and the unity and integrity of the Nation;

IN OUR CONSTITUENT ASSEMBLY this twenty-sixth day of November, 1949, do HEREBY ADOPT, ENACT AND GIVE TO OURSELVES THIS CONSTITUTION?

Syntactic Interpretation of the Preamble

The long compound sentence is divided into various parts with the commas and semicolons. The adjectives *SOVEREIGN, SOCIALIST, SECULAR, DEMOCRATIC, REPUBLIC* have been used in the beginning show alliteration with the repetition of the sound 's'. Further, the aims are stated which are further explained with more adjectives. So *JUSTICE* is *social, economic and political.* There is a marked break with a semicolon as equally important points follow. It is the oath to secure *LIBERTY* of *thought, expression, belief, faith and worship*. Again with a semicolon yet another point is noted down-*EQUALITY of status and of opportunity;* and to promote among them all. One more point is eminent and it is the last one-*FRATERNITY assuring the dignity of the individual and the unity and integrity of the Nation*. Though the sentences are divided by the semicolons and breaks in the lines, the sense is continuous and many things are covered in the briefest possible way. The words are stately, the composition of the preamble is of epic scale, the style is also grave and the overall form of it is elevated. There is parallelism in the structure. Firstly the adjectives are having the same form and then the important points which substantiate the constitution. Hence, we find *justice, liberty, equality and fraternity* are have parallel structure. Interestingly their form is same. All the letters of these core words are capital letters and they are foregrounded and highlighted through that. Moreover, the nouns *justice, liberty, equality and fraternity* have been followed by the adjectives that describe and qualify the nouns that they follow. This parallelism in the structure at once makes it easy to understand and looks great in form and appearance. The syntactic structures, the tight and compact sentence structure, the systematic division of the sentence make the preamble at once an embellished piece of writing and a superb example of rhetoric.

The preamble of the Indian constitution vehemently shows that the length matters little if the sentence is systematically drafted and properly divided.

The Syntax of/in Acts:

The Acts have a very typical syntax. It has been very systematically drafted with the delineation of minute details. Utmost care and caution is taken besides each and every necessary term is duly explained. Moreover, citations are given to refer to the precedents.

Ambiguity in Legal Language:

Inactive and ambiguous form of words can create doubt in legal result for example, the expression: "*Notice shall be issued.*" It is not categorically mentioned who will issue the notice. Here is another expression: "School building shall have fire alarms." It is not clear as to who the issuing authority is and who would be liable-School Authority; Fire Brigade, State Fire Extinguisher Office or the Electrical Contractor.

An Impersonal and Detached Style of Writing:

Using passive forms is one of the most common methods of emphasizing the impersonal in a language (Sarcevic 177). The comprehensive use of the third person (singular and plural) in legislative texts helps to emphasize the idea of objectivity, detachment and authoritativeness. Where, for instance, a provision applies to everybody, the sentence either begins with every person, everyone etc.

No one may be subjected to slavery, servitude or forced labour.

Everyone has the right of access to- (a) any information held by the state; and (b) any information that is held by another person and that is required for the exercise or protection of any rights.

On the other hand in wills, which is a personalized document, the first person singular is used abundantly. One of the few exceptions to the common rule of 'impersonalization' in legislative texts is usually seen at the beginning of constitutional documents, such as the Preamble to the Indian Constitution where the first-person plural pronoun and possessive adjective are used:

"WE, THE PEOPLE OF INDIA, having solemnly resolved to constitute India into a SOVEREIGN SOCIALIST SECULAR

DEMOCRATIC REPUBLIC and to secure to all its citizens..." (Wikipedia)

Verbosity:

Another important feature of legal language is verbosity. Verbosity or verboseness refers to speech or writing which uses more words than needed. Precision and conciseness are the hallmarks of good writing style. Verbosity is writing considered as a defect, where one word can suffice, why there is the necessity of many? This is a common question that arises in the minds of readers. There are varieties of expressions and variety is the spice of life. The word "although' has its verbose expression in the form of a phrase 'despite the fact that'.

The drafters of legal language have been often criticized for their verbose expressions. There are literary figures like Mark Twain and Ernest Hemingway who are known for their terse styles and evading verbosity. Wordiness, circumlocution, prolixity, grandiloquence, and volubility are the associates of verbosity and all are detested. "Slang terms such as verbal diarrhea also refer to the practice." (Wikipedia)

Often, to express one view, two or three words are used differently and rather unnecessarily. The following comparison of the verbose and exact expression justifies the same:

Verbose Expression	**Exact Expression**
Give consideration to	consider
Give goods to	delivery
At the time of his birth	when he was born
Have need of	need
Make provision for	provide (for)

The legalistic and ordinary expressions also make a vast difference in understanding:

Legalistic	Ordinary
Adequate number of	enough
Be empowered to	may
Be able to	can
Abutting	next
Per diem	per day
In case	if
Previous to	before
Pursuant to	in accordance with
Until such time as	until
In order to	to
In the interest of	for
Per annum	per year

The verbose expressions increase the complexity of the legal expression. Use of redundant wording where a shorter and clearer expression would convey the same legal meaning reduces clarity rather than enhancing precision. This verboseness is often results in leaving gaps and loopholes in the interpretation and elucidation of law.

The loquacious wordiness and redundancy have been severely criticized even by the persons belonging to the legal sector. It has been further disapproved that the motto of the law fraternity seems to be "Never use one word where you can use two; and the more you use, the better". Verbosity is evident at many instances. Nevertheless, verbose is commonly found in the grants of rights. It has been said that the grantee is given "the full right to pass and repass on foot or with or without vehicles along and over the foot paths and roads respectively of the said estate". (J&K State Land Grants Act, 1960)

Use of prepositional phrases:

The use of prepositional phrases in particular and other phrases in general also leads to verbose or wordiness. Prepositional phrases are preferred to adverbs which demands addition of extra words to be added and contribute to verbosity.

Instead of using the subordinators like 'if, 'before', and 'after', the phrases such as 'in the event that', 'prior to', or 'subsequent to' have been preferred. Instead of using 'during', 'during the time that' has been used whereas in place of 'until', 'until such time as' and in place of 'to', 'in order to' for 'to' have been employed which increase the complexity and contribute to wordiness.

There have been many examples in India and abroad where lengthiness is evident in the law books, pleadings and judgments. There has been a recent example of lengthiness caused by wordiness wherein a pleading which was originally of over 2600 pages had to be reduced to about 360 pages. The judge expressed his dislike and displeasure at it by using epithets like "contradictory, embarrassing, and so convoluted that the pleadings are well-nigh impossible... to comprehend."

(South Australia Vs Peat Marwick Mitchell & Co.)

An American expert on legal language Richard Wydick who advocated clarity opines:

"Lawyers are busy, cautious people, and they cannot afford to make mistakes. The old, redundant phrases worked in the past, a new one may somehow raise a question. To check it in the law library will take time and time is the lawyer's most precious commodity. But remember once you stay one of these old monsters, it will stay dead for the rest of your legal career. Such trophies distinguish a lawyer from scrivener." (20-21)

Latinism in Legal Language:

Legalese is full of the Latin lexicon. Not just words but the Latin phrases represent a distinct identity of legal syntax. The English equivalents or the English meaning of the Latin expressions are different obviously, problems are faced while interpreting the Latin expressions. Here are some examples of the Latin phrases used extensively in the legal language.

ad hoc for	this purpose
amicus curiae	friend of the court
bona fide	in good faith
corpus delicti	"body of the crime"-material evidence that crime has occurred
cui bono	good for whom, i.e., who benefits?
de facto	according to the fact or deed
de jure	according to the law
de minimis non	
curat lex	the law takes no account of trifles
et uxor	and (his) wife
ex officio	by virtue of the office held
ex post facto	a new law applied retroactively to a deed already done
habeas corpus	you may have the body (writ requiring party be brought to court promptly)

mala fide	in bad faith
in flagrante delicto	in the act
in prope persona	in one's own person without a lawyer
ipso facto	by the very deed
modus operandi	manner of working, operating
nolo prosequi	"I don't wish to prosecute" (will drop all parts of a lawsuit)
nolo contendere	I will not contend (plea equal to admission of guilt but allows recourse to deny the matter in subsequent proceedings)
non compos mentis	not of sane mind
obiter dictum	a judicial opinion not binding on other courts
onus probandi	burden of proof
per se	in itself
prima facie	at first sight
pro forma	as a matter of form only
pro tempore (pro tem)	for the time being, temporarily
quid pro quo exchange	something for something a fair
sine die	without a specific date set for reconvening
subpoena	under (threat of) punishment

Equivocal Expressions:

"Equivocation is the use of ambiguous language with the purpose of avoiding telling the truth or committing oneself". (New Oxford American Dictionary) Having several meanings, synonymous with ambiguous. The word equivocal is an adjective and has number of synonyms which shows its complexity and extensive use in the legal discourse. Here is the list of the synonyms:

- ambiguous
- ambivalent
- amphibological
- bewildering
- cloudy
- confusing
- controversial
- debatable
- deceptive
- dim
- disputable
- doubtful
- dubious
- enigmatic
- enigmatical
- equivocating
- equivocatory
- hard to understand

- hazy
- imprecise
- indecisive
- indefinite
- indeterminate
- misleading
- moot
- nebulous
- obscure
- of doubtful meaning
- of uncertain significance
- open
- open to question
- perplexing
- possessing double meaning
- prevaricating
- puzzling
- questionable
- recondite
- shadowy
- uncertain
- unclarified
- unclear

- undecided
- undefined
- undetermined
- unexplained
- unintelligible
- unresolved
- unsolved
- unsure
- untransparent
- vague

Nominalization:

Equivocal words and those which are used in a doubtful sense are to be understood in their more worthy and effective sense

Nominalization has been perceived as either a lexical or a syntactic device in literature. As far as its lexical sense is concerned, it has been defined as "a process whereby a verb or adjective is converted into a noun" (Givon 287), whereas in a broader in general and syntactic sense in particular, it is "the process via which a prototypical verbal clause, either a complete one (including the subject) or a verb phrase (excluding the subject), is converted into a noun phrase" *(ibid.)*.

Legal discourse is full of nominalizations. It is a distinct feature of the legal language but at the same time it is profanity on the part of the layperson or the average-common reader. Nominalizations let the speaker to leave out reference to the performer. Here is an example of publishing agreement where nominalization is reasonable:

Many linguists have advocated the judicious use of nominalization. They believe that through nominalization, information can be condensed in titles, lists and preambles, and can systematically arranged as a series of nominal expressions so as to fit well with the organized structure of parliamentary acts and articles. Nominalization conforms to some of the primary requirements of legal writing, namely efficiency and concision on the one hand, and condensation and all-inclusiveness on the other hand.

Encapsulation is one of the important aspect of nominalization. Nominalization enables to create the sense of objectivity and makes the text more ambiguous. In a text packed with nominalizations, when clausal patterns or consistent forms are replaced by nominalized ones, some of the information is lost. Nominalization sometimes makes the wording more lengthy, complex, objective, succinct, convincing, and unified. It is best to use straightforward, direct and candid active verbs rather than nominalizations or passives. The basic sentence type containing a subject, active verbs and object, is easiest for people to process. (Fredrick Bowers 339).

The Auxiliary and the Main Verb:

Separation of the helping verb from its main verb is another characteristic feature of the legal syntax. The following examples will suffice the view:

a. ... the vendor if called upon to do *so will* at the request of the purchaser or any person deriving title under him, *do* all lawful assurances

b. The Insured *shall* within fourteen days of the loss or damage coming to his knowledge and at his own expense *deliver* to the company a claim in writing containing as particular an account as may be reasonably practicable. (Victoria A.)

Because of this feature, it is often very difficult to comprehend the legal text without efforts. It increases the complexity and the layperson may find it too difficult to understand easily.

Use of combinational Phrases:

It has been noticed in the legal texts that the sentences in the legal texts are full of numerous clauses and phrases. There are plenty of adjective phrases, noun phrases, prepositional and adverbial, finite and non-finite clauses, and of-constructions.

The commonly found legal prepositional phrases are 'In the event of', 'for a period of, and 'during the course of. However, it is because of the convention that they have been retained otherwise they can be substituted by the words. Words replacing the phrases can minimize wordiness and subsequently the sentence length and consequently the complexity. The shortened forms of prepositional phrases can be as follows:

'In the event of' = 'if',

'For a period of' = 'for'.

'During the course of' = 'during'.

Many words carry both literal and idiomatic meanings. They may be termed as the connotative and denotative meanings. The words and phrases in ordinary usage may mean differently from their use in the legal senses.

Here are some more prepositional phrases with their simplified equivalents preferred by the proponents and practitioners of plain English taken from Bryan *Garner's Legal Writing in Plain English (2013)* an adequate number of - enough

a number of - many/several

a sufficient number of - enough

at the present time - now

at the time when - when

at this point in time - now

during such time as - while

for the reason that - because

in the near future - soon

is able to - can

notwithstanding the fact that - although

on a daily basis - daily

on the ground that - because

prior to - before

subsequent to - after

the majority of - most

until such time as – until

Chapter-3

The Role and Relevance of Legal Lexicon

The legal lexicon captures the spirit and soul of every legal document. A precise knowledge and clear understanding of legal vocabulary can lay a strong foundation of effective legal drafting, analysis and interpretation. Legal language relies on exact word choice and the usage consequently affects the outcome in the form of opinions and judicial decisions.

The Use of the Modal Auxiliaries 'Shall' and 'May' :

Shall denotes obligation and is also customarily used to communicate an obligatory or mandatory outcome of a legal decision. The word 'Shall' is frequently used as the most powerful imperative expression. It is not just a marker of the future tense but also an imperative marker. It denotes something which is compulsory, final and without any alternative. E.g. *"A person appointed as Member shall hold office for a term of five years from the date on which he enters upon his office."* (Chitnis 84) It is used for something obligatory and if not 'may' is used for permission.

As opined in *State of UP v. Manbodhan Lal Srivastava* (SC Nirnay Patrika 606) that the meaning of the word 'shall' in any statute is interpreted as mandatory, but is not it necessary that it is always used in mandatory sense. Traditionally, the modal shall, in legal texts, carries an obligation or a duty as opposed to its common function: expressing futurity (Tiersma 105)

Usually, 'shall' denotes command and 'may' denotes permission and possibility. But in the legalese in general and in statues in particular 'shall' makes it directory and not mandatory, e.g. 'shall be accepted', 'notice shall be given'. It is synonymous to the expression 'may be'. Sometimes other modal auxiliaries like *must* and *would* are also used. 'Shall' has a special function in statutes. It has been used to indicate something that is intended to be legally compulsory or binding. This also makes it unambiguous. Frederick Bowers has rightly noted that 'shall' is generally "used as a kind of totem, to conjure up some flavour of the law". (80)

Use of Quotidian Words:

It is difficult to decode and distinguish the literal meaning with figurative (suggesting) meaning in legal language. Legal discourse some-words have different meaning in legalese which makes the context little more intricate, such words differ in meaning from the ordinary-everyday discourse. The words e.g., *action* (lawsuit), *consideration* (support for a promise), *execute* (to sign to effect), and *party* (a principal in a lawsuit) are commonly used in the legalese. There are other words like *right, suit, duty, wrong, contract, necessary, arbitrary* which have dual meanings.

Some Quotidian words extensively used in law books

Action : not a physical movement, but a lawsuit.

Brief : a noun referring to a type of legal document, not an adjective, and despite the name, virtually never brief.

Continuance : the postponement of a proceeding until a later date; if a judge continues a hearing, it will not continue, but will stop and start up again later.

Notice : formally notifying a person of something, as in giving notice of a claim against that person. It is legally effective, as a rule,

	regardless of whether anybody actually notices it.
Personal property:	Property other than real property, including not only used clothing and furniture, but also automobiles and large trucks.
*Praye*r :	usually the last part of the pleading in which the party requests the court to grant or deny the relief sought by the plaintiff.

Tandon and Behl are of the opinion that "Lawyers are partial to typical legalistic words like adjacent to, contiguous to, forthwith intimate, subsequent to, pursuant to etc." they further expose the defects in the legalese saying "The legal draftsman shares a special affinity with certain words.

Lawyers 'execute' rather than sign; they insist on 'shall' when it means 'must'." (8)

Interpretation is a very important thing in legal discourse. Words do not carry same meaning in all the situations. Certain words have distinctive meanings in legal contexts. We are here reminded of Lord Macmillan who emphasizes the golden rule of interpretation that "the grammatical and ordinary sense of the word is to be adhered to unless that would lead to some absurdity or some repugnance or inconsistency with the rest of the instrument, in which case the grammatical or ordinary sense of the word may be modified so as to avoid that absurdity and inconsistency but no further." (quoted, Tandon & Behl 4)

Legal language is characterized by the words or expressions with general or sometimes flexible meanings. It has been believed that such terminology is used for its flexibility. It has been taken quite positively. Reed Dickerson (48) notes that flexibility in legal language is often a "positive benefit". The best example of such flexible words is the word 'reasonable' which has been exploited and at times misused quite often in the legal language. We find it in the expressions like 'reasonable care', 'beyond a reasonable doubt' and 'reasonable man'. A foremost American commentator on law William Prosser (15) has said:

"The conduct of the reasonable man will vary with the situation with which he is confronted; under the latitude of this phrase, the courts have made allowance and have applied, in many respects, a less subjective standard." The Recurrence of certain words and expressions, flexible words and doublets enhances precision and helps to maintain consistency and clarity by reinforcing the meaning.

The Use of Doublets:

One of the salient features of legalese is legal doublet. Doublets are the words which are used in pairs. They can be termed as word pairs. They are "fixed in the mind as frozen expressions, typically irreversible" (Danet 281). Their root can be traced in the Norman Period. "A legal doublet is a standardized phrase used frequently in English legal language consisting of two or more words that are near synonyms." (Wikipedia). Following are some of the examples arranged in an alphabetical order:

- Able and willing
- aid and abet
- all and sundry
- acknowledge and confess
- alter or change
- answerable and accountable
- appropriate and proper
- art and part

- attach and annex
- bills and notes
- bind and obligate
- breaking and entering
- by and between
- care and attention
- cease and desist
- covenant and agree
- custom and usage
- deem and consider
- demise and lease
- depose and say
- devise and bequeath
- due and payable
- due and owing
- each and every
- final and conclusive
- fit and proper
- fraud and deceit
- free and clear
- from now and henceforth
- full faith and credit
- furnish and supply

- good and tenable
- goods and chattels
- have and hold
- heirs and successors
- hue and cry
- indemnify and hold harmless
- just and equitable
- keep and perform
- keep and maintain
- kind and nature
- law and order
- legal and valid
- let or hindrance
- lewd and lascivious conduct.
- liens and encumbrances
- maintenance and upkeep
- make and enter into
- means and includes
- mind and memory
- new and novel
- null and void
- over and above
- part and parcel

- peace and quiet
- perform and discharge are used as a stylistic and
- power and authority
- restrain and enjoin
- sale or transfer
- separate and apart
- sole and exclusive
- successor and assigns
- surmise and conjecture are commonly
- terms and conditions
- then and in that event
- true and correct
- understood and agreed
- unless and until
- various and sundry
- will and testament
- cancel, annul and set aside

Use of Triplets in legalese:-

Triplets are near synonyms used as one unit to convey a specific Legal concept. They are used as a stylistic and rhetorical device to emphasize legal meaning, ensure clarity and to avoid ambiguity, Triplets are commonly used in statutes, contracts, pleadings, legal drafting, in court judgments to ensure that all legal nuances are covered.

Common legal triplets used in legalese:

- Arbitrary, capricious, and unreasonable.
- convey, transfer and set over
- form, manner and method
- give, devise and bequeath
- grant, bargain, sell
- lands, tenements and hereditaments
- name, constitute and appoint
- ordered, adjudged and decreed
- possession, custody and control
- remise, release and forever quit claim
- ready, willing and able
- repair, hold and maintain
- rest, residue and remainder
- right, title and interest

Doublets are but the repetition of the same word in another form. The words are synonymous most of the times and hence, repetition of any kind brings monotony. The scholars believed that because of the doublets, the legal language becomes clearer and easier for the understanding of the users, However, many modern legal scholars and writers speak against the doublets and triplets and advise to eliminate them altogether because they feel that doublets and triplets are unnecessarily superfluous and/or redundant.

Use of 'Any' as a term of broad inclusion

In legal language, the word 'any' is very common and is often used as a term of broad inclusion to broaden the scope of a clause, obligation, or prohibition. The expressions like *any child or children* any person who trespasses, *encumbrances, and other assets, etc* are found in plenty.

Use of Argot:-

Argot refers to a specialized set of vocabulary or jargon which is used by a particular group. Such words are often used to create barrier to legal communication and establishes exclusive identity of specific terms. Argot is at times known as the insider language, familiar to a particular group. Some of the examples of argot are inferior court, contributory negligence, due care, mens rea, voir dire, charge, bar, bench, Miranda etc. Legal Argot helps the legal professionals to communicate quickly and precisely but can lead to confusion for the defendants and the public.

Use of Open Textured words:-

The Terms or impressions whose meaning is now precisely defined and the usage may very as per the judicial discretion are commonly known as open-textured words in Law: For eg- gross negligence, reasonable person, undue influence, good cause, just and equitable public interest, justice, due care etc. These are deliberately flexible terms of law which can be adapted to different situations for interpreting law. The judges can interpret these terms based on context, fats, and social norms and values. Introduced by H.L.A. Hart, these open –textured words allows the legal experts to adapt to new and unforeseen situations and to apply discretion with utmost care.

Use of Repetitive and Resonant Words:-

Legal language is full of repetitive and resonant words for the purpose of clarity, emphasis and legal effect. In legal drafting, the deliberate use of repetitive words serves a vital function in promoting clarity, precision, and legal certainty. Rather than employing synonyms, legal drafters often repeat terms to remove ambiguity and minimize the risk of divergent interpretations by courts. Such repetition ensures consistency across statutes, contracts, and other legal instruments, guaranteeing that specific terminology retains a uniform meaning throughout. Classic examples include formulations such as "null and void," "cease and desist," "each and every," and "fit and proper," where paired or reiterated words reinforce completeness, obligation, and enforceability. The repeated use of modal verbs such as "shall" similarly underscores mandatory duties. While this practice may appear redundant in ordinary discourse, in the legal context it is a purposeful strategy designed to safeguard against misinterpretation and to preclude potential loopholes.

Formal Utterances:-

There are many bygone practices still in vogue on the legal sphere. The typical colonial practice of addressing the Court as the '*Honourable Court*', Counsel is referred as the '*learned counsel*', and a Judge is reverently called as '*Your Honour*' and so on. In India, the use of the expression "My Lord" in courts has largely been discouraged. The Supreme Court of India and several High Courts have advised the advocates to avoid colonial-era forms of address such as "My Lord" or "Your Lordship" and instead use neutral and respectful terms consistent with constitutional values. The preferred forms of address today are "Your Honour" or "Honourable Court", which are considered appropriate in both the Supreme Court and High Courts. Although "My Lord" may still occasionally be heard, especially from senior members of the Bar, it is not the recommended practice, and advocates are encouraged to adopt the modern forms. If such expressions are not used, it is considered derogatory and disrespectful.

Chapter-4
Adverbials and Determiners

Another unique feature of the legal lexicon is the blend of the adverbials of place and prepositions to form adverbials. Adverbials are words, phrases, or clauses that add extra information to a sentence by modifying a verb, an adjective, another adverb, or even the whole sentence. They typically answer questions such as how, when, where, why, how often, or to what extent an action takes place. For example, in the sentence "The judge carefully considered the evidence," the adverbial carefully explains how the action was done, while in "The case was heard yesterday," yesterday shows time. Adverbials may take different forms, including single adverbs (quickly), prepositional phrases (in the courtroom), or clauses (because the matter was urgent). They can be placed at the beginning, middle, or end of a sentence, depending on emphasis and clarity. In formal and academic writing, adverbials should be used thoughtfully to improve precision and coherence without making sentences vague or wordy. Adverbials are formed in plenty in the legal discourse and a few of them have been used in the ordinary usage too. For example-

- whereof
- wherein
- hereto
- hereon
- hereby
- hereof
- herein

- hereinbefore
- hereinafter
- therein
- thereafter
- thereto
- therewith
- thereat
- thereunder
- therefor
- thereon
- thereupon
- hereunder
- therefrom
- thereof

Such words were quite common in medieval English. Instead of saying 'under it' or 'under that', medieval English speaker would say 'hereunder' or 'thereunder'. These adverbials help to obtain precise references in the legal discourse. In legal writing many common archaic terms act as a specific type of adverbial known as pronomial adverbs e.g. ‘herein’, ‘thereof’’, whereby etc.

The Use of Special Determiners:

In legal language, determiners play a vital role in ensuring precision and avoiding ambiguity. Their careful use can significantly affect legal interpretation. For example, the definite article “the” is used to refer to a specific and clearly identified person or thing, as in “the accused,” “the contract,” or “the court,” indicating that the reference is limited to the entity already defined. In contrast, the indefinite articles "a" or "an" introduce a non-specific reference and are often interpreted to mean "any" or "one or more," as in "a witness may be examined," "a license shall be granted," or "a director may convene a meeting," which can broaden legal scope. Quantifying determiners such as "each" and "every" emphasize inclusiveness and individual application, as seen in "each party shall comply with its obligations" and "every employee must adhere to company policy." Broad determiners like "any" and restrictive ones like "no" are frequently used to widen or limit legal consequences, for example, "any breach of this agreement shall result in termination" and "no amendment shall be valid unless made in writing."

Demonstrative determiners such as "this" and "that" commonly refer to the document itself, as in "this agreement shall come into force on the date of execution," while the determiner "such" links a provision to a previously stated concept, as in "such failure shall constitute a material breach."

Possessive determiners like "its" and "their" further clarify responsibility and ownership, for instance, "the company shall fulfill its statutory duties" and "the parties shall bear their respective costs." Together, these examples show how determiners in legal drafting are used deliberately to define scope, assign liability, and ensure clarity.

Nominalization:

Nominalization is a salient feature of legal nominalization. It is used to add a formal tone of expression by constructing abstract legal concepts which makes legal language more complex.

Nominalization is both a lexical and a syntactic feature of legal language. In the lexical sense it can be defined as a process where a verb or adjective is converted into a noun. Quirk (Quirk et al. 1985) considers that nominalization is a process or turning a verb or an adjective into a noun. Nominalization has been defined as the grammatical process of forming nouns from other parts of speech, usually verbs or adjectives. According to Chomsky (1968), "nominalization is a process by which a stem, verb phrase, or sentence is transformed into a nominal". Thompson in his book Reading and discrimination has said that (167), nominalization is the use of nominal form a root word, an attributive meaning or a relational process together with the Attribute".

In legal texts deverbal nominalization is extensively used where the suffixes *'ion'* and *'ment'* are found in abundance. We have the nominalised words with the suffix ion like *foundation, protection, provision, adoption, discrimination, consideration, and implementation* and with the suffix *ment* such as *development, punishment, imprisonment, agreement, involvement, enjoyment*. The suffixes *ion* and *ment* consign the state, action or instance of verbs and indicate the process of making or doing.

Examples of the nominalizations frequently found in legalese:-

- give consideration of = consider
- give recognition to= recognize
- have knowledge of = know
- have a need of = need
- in the determination of = in determining
- is applicable = applies
- is dependent on = depends on
- is in attendance at = attends
- make an appointment of = appoint

- make application = apply
- make payment = pay
- make provision for = provide for

Examples of nominalization through the nominalizers – 'or' and '-ee':-

Assign refers to

- *assignor :* (a person from whom a property or a right is legally transferred)
- *assignee:* (a person to whom a property or a right is legally transferred)
- Transfer refers to
- *transferor:* (a person from whom a property or the deed drawn from it is conveyed)
- *transferee :* (a person to whom a property or the deed drawn from it is conveyed) Mortgage refers to
- *mortgagor:* (a debtor who gives his property in a mortgage)
- *mortgagee*: (a creditor who receives a mortgage) (Victoria A. Alabi)

The suffix *-or* which designates **one who gives** and the suffix *-ee* which designates **one who receives** are used differently in the legal discourse. In the following examples, the lexemes with asterisk are exclusively found in the legalese and not in general English:

inspector *inspectee

survivor *survive

*appointor =appointee

However, the words like *employer-employee* and *addresser-addressee* are commonly found in both the legalese and the general

English. When a verb is converted to a noun, the sentence requires additional verbs, prepositions and articles which make the legalese full of verbose. Nominalizations also tend to lead to passive voice and weaker verb choice. Nominalizations also adds wordiness to the sentence structures and even elaborates sentence structure.

Unusual Use of the Words 'The Same', 'Such' And 'Said':

One of the most common and ancient legalism in legal language is the use of the word 'said'. It has been used differently in different situations. It is used as an article or demonstrative pronoun: John promises to pay a deposit. Said deposit shall accrue interest at a rate of five percent per annum. (J&K Houses and Shops Rent Control Act. 1966.)

In the above instance, the definite article 'the' or the demonstrative pronoun 'this' could replace 'said' and facilitate ease on the part of the reader. In an ordinary sense, 'Said' is also used as an adjective: the said deposit is equally possible. It appears archaic too. Tiersma opines that the word 'said' could be substituted by the article 'the' or the demonstrative pronoun 'this' with no loss of meaning. The words the same, such and said have distinct identity in the legal discourse. The word 'the same usually implies comparison to a similar object or person, but in legal use it refers to sameness of reference. In order to support the idea, the following example has been served:

'The tenant shall pay all the taxes regularly levied and assessed against Premises and keep the same in repair". (88)

In the above cited example, the word 'premises' has been refereed or substituted by 'the same which, according to Tiersma, can be done by the personal pronoun 'it'.(91) 'It' seems to be a more convenient option.

A close variant of 'said' is aforesaid. It is almost similar in meaning as 'said', because anything said 'before' or 'afore'. According to David Mellinkoff, "the purpose of 'aforesaid is to refer to something that has been said, and its chief vice is that you can't be sure what it refers to", 'Said' and 'aforesaid' are exclusively anaphoric, as they can only refer to something that has been mentioned previously. Actually said' and 'aforesaid' are literal translations from Latin terms, 'dictus', 'said' and 'predictus', 'aforesaid'. (340)

Besides 'the same', 'such' is another unusual word found in plenty in the legal language. As far as the usual or general use of such' is concerned, it means 'that sort' or 'this sort''.

"We conclude that the trial court's order constituted an abuse of discretion in the procedural posture of this case which compels us to set aside such order."(SLJ.)

In the above cited example, 'such order' means 'this (exact) order'. It seems that, the phrase 'such order' denotes 'this order. Therefore, *Such* acts similar to the demonstrative pronoun *this.* Moreover, employment of 'such' confuses because it has the possibility of being interpreted to mean 'this kind of (especially in the plural).

"Lessee promises to pay a deposit. Said deposit shall accrue interest at a rate of five percent per annum."

Lexical repetition or redundancy:-

Anaphoric devices or referential pronouns are mostly avoided in the legal language. The example is of the personal pronouns (he, she, it and so on) or the demonstrative ones (this, that, these and those) besides the verb "to do' which may help to substitute a whole clause as evident in:

Legal Jargon and Judicial Expressions:-

Jargon refers to a language which is used in a specific context and may not be well understood outside of it nor have much significance to a lay man. It refers to the special vocabulary of a profession that distinguishes it from the other fields. Legal jargon denotes the specialized and technical vocabulary employed within the legal profession to articulate rights, obligations, procedures, and principles with precision. It is designed to ensure clarity, consistency, and legal certainty in statutes, contracts, and judicial decisions. However, due to its formal structure, historical roots, and reliance on technical and Latin-derived terms, legal jargon may be difficult for non-legal readers to comprehend, underscoring the importance of clear drafting and, where appropriate, the use of plain language to enhance accessibility without compromising legal accuracy. This special vocabulary that is expected to be understood by the persons belonging to the profession is termed as jargon. Precisely explaining, Jargon refers to words and phrases used by a particular group of people, especially in their profession, that are not generally understood by others. Black's Law Dictionary clearly defines legal jargon as "the specialialized or technical terminology characteristic of the legal profession, often unintelligible to those outside the field".

Legal Jargon is inherently rooted in the historical terminology derived from Latin and Greek language. The use of legal Jargon allows the law students, scholars, lawyers and judges to draft and structure legal documents with more precision and clarity of thoughts. Jargon lends a formal tone to the legal communication, avoids ambiguity, and reinforces the authority of legal tents.

Jargon is thus "the technical terminology or characteristic idiom of a special activity or group". (Wikipedia) Some of the examples of legal jargon are 'black-letter law', 'boilerplate', 'case at bar', 'case on point', 'case on all fours', 'chilling effect', 'conclusory', 'decedent', grandfather clause', 'a hypothetical (used as a noun, as in a good hypothetical is hard to find), 'instant case', 'judge shopping', and numerous others.

Precision clarity and efficiency of communication are the main aims targeted by the jargon. The widely accepted and extensively used words are retained so as to give specific meaning which helps to avoid circumlocution. However, all this is done at the cost of simplicity and comprehensibility.

Bassey Garvey and Ufot in a scholarly paper *'Use of Jargon* '(6-7) classifies jargon as true jargon and pseudo jargon.

The following examples have been given in the scholarly paper:

A. True Jargon

1. addendum (Latin) an addition; something added
2. affidavit (Latin) a written declaration made upon oath
3. alias (Latin) an assumed name
4. alibi (Latin) the excuse of being elsewhere when a crime was committed.
5. arson (Old French; Latin) a crime of willfully setting fire to property for purposes of mischief
6. assault (Old French; Latin) an intentional or reckless act which results in immediate and unlawful violence to another
7. bail (Old French; Latin) money for temporary release of a suspect who must appear in court or it is forfeited
8. battery (Old French; Latin) unlawful physical violence against a person
9. defendant (Old French; Latin) a person against whom a court action is brought
10. equity (Old French; Latin) decisions based on principles of natural justice and fair conduct

11. exhibit (Latin) a document or object produced as evidence in court
12. felony (Old French; Latin) a (serious) crime
13. fiduciary (Latin) trustee; a person who acts on behalf of another in relation to his beneficiary
14. homicide (Old French: Latin) the killing of a human being by another person
15. libel (Old French; Latin) a written offensive material considered injurious or defamatory of another person
16. lien (Old French; Latin) right to retain possession of another's property pending the discharge of a debt
17. litigate (Latin) to bring a lawsuit
18. manslaughter (Old English) the accidental killing of another human being
19. murder (Old English: Latin) the unlawful and willful killing of another human being
20. perjury (Old French; Latin) the offence of giving false evidence under oath in court
21. plaintiff (Old French) a person who brings a civil action
22. proviso (Latin) a clause containing a condition; a condition
23. quash (Old French; Latin) to make void or invalid; cancel
24. res (Latin) matter; issue or object
25. slander (Old French; Latin) a spoken offensive material considered injurious or defamatory of another person
26. subpoena (Latin) under penalty; a writ issued by a court requiring a person to appear in court
27. tort (Old French; Latin) a wrong arising from an act of commission or omission without regard to a contract
28. treason (Old French; Latin) betrayal of, or crime against, one's country

29. trespass (Old French; Latin) to intrude or encroach on another person's private property, privacy and rights
30. writ (Old English) a sealed document ordering a person to do, or refrain from doing, some specified act

It is interesting to note that much of the words mentioned above are derived from Latin. They are retained for giving precision and stability in the meaning. Bassey and Garvey distinguished between true jargon and pseudo-jargon in professional and legal language. True jargon consists of specialized terms that are essential for precise and unambiguous communication within a profession, such as prima facie, indemnify, or hereinafter in legal contexts. These terms serve a clear functional purpose, allowing experts to convey complex concepts efficiently. In contrast, pseudo-jargon refers to language that appears technical or sophisticated but is unnecessary, vague, or used primarily to impress rather than clarify. Such language often obscures meaning, complicating understanding without adding precision. In essence, true jargon enhances professional communication, while pseudo-jargon merely complicates it.

Bassey and Garvey Ufot (7) also mentions that the words like manslaughter, murder, quash and trespass, which have been termed as true jargon have no exact English equivalents. He also believes that morphologically most of such (legal words) lexical terms have no affixes reinforcing their ease of pronunciation. In order to focus on the syllabic structure of such lexical items, it has been found that there is noticeable division of words with two and three syllables. The following charts illustrates the division:

Monosyllables	Dissyllables	Trisyllables	Polysyllables
bail	alias	addendum	affidavit
lien	arson	alibi	fiduciary
quash	assault	defendant	
res	battery	equity	
tort	libel	exhibit	
writ	murder	felony	
	plaintiff	homicide	
	slander	litigate	
	treason	manslaughter	
	trespass	perjury	
		proviso	
		subpoena	

B. Pseudo-jargon

The lexical items that no more appear to be jargon because of their extensive use in legalese are termed as pseudo jargon. Bassey and Garvey Ufot (8-9) lists ten popular pseudo jargon:-

1. ab initio (Latin) from the start
2. amicus curiae (Latin) friend of the court; a person who is not directly involved in a case but advises the court
3. ex parte (Latin) motion or injunction on behalf of one party only in a court case
4. habeas corpus (Latin) you have the body; an order for a detainee to be brought to court
5. interlocutory injunction (from Latin) a provisional pronouncement in the course of court proceedings

6. locus standi (Latin) a place for standing; the right of a party to appear and be heard in court
7. mens rea (Latin) guilty mind; a criminal intention or knowledge that an act is wrong
8. pari passu (Latin) with equal speed or progress; the right of creditors to receive assets equally from the source
9. prima facie (Latin) at first sight; evidence as it seems at first
10. sub judice (Latin) under judicial consideration; a rule which makes it an offence to make comments which might prejudice a case in court

It can be seen from the above list that there is predominance of the Latin-origin words besides the words or lexical items from Old French which constitute the legal lexicon.

Chapter-5
The Technical and the Archaic Language

The etymological features of legal language are integral to understand the technical aspects of legalese. A lexicon is the vocabulary of a person, language, or branch of knowledge. A legal lexicon is a systematically organized compendium of legal terms and expressions, defined with precision, interpreted within the framework of statutory law, judicial precedent and doctrine. Legal lexicon has its own characteristics. It differs from the general-usual discourse in multiple ways. Three p's namely, 'precision', 'preservation' and 'prestige' are quite crucial in this regard. Legal language is characterized by utmost precision as every care is taken to avoid gaps. The archaic words from the traditional sources have been used in the legal texts, since long and are available in the forms of treaties, contracts, agreements, etc. they are known as legal jargon today as they belong to the classical languages like Greek and Latin. The legal drafters also prefer such words in the legal documents as the retaining of the words does not necessarily change the connotations or acquire new meanings of the words utilized. The words from such sources have validity for years and hence the necessity of new words does not arise.

Thomas Jefferson, lawyer and statesman had criticized the legal language in general, particularly words for the reason that language becomes incomprehensible due to the use of *saids, ands, ors* and *aforesaid.* According to him the excessive length of sentences in legal documents leads to complexity.

In the practice of law, 'words are the tools of trade', as said by Lord Denning. The specialized vocabulary referred to as legal lexicon serves as the foundation of all legal communication whether verbal and non-verbal. Embedded with institutional practice, interpretive tradition and jurisprudential vocabulary the legal lexicon reflects the conceptual structure and historical evolution of legal thoughts. Lord Denning in his Book, 'The Discipline of Law' quoted:

> "To succeed in the profession of the law, you must seek to cultivate command of language. Words are the lawyer's tools of trade. When you are called upon to address a judge, it is your words which count most. It is by them thar you will hope to persuade the judge of the righrness of your cause". (Denning, 5)

Jefferson attacked the endless tautologies, convulsion of case within case, parenthesis with parenthesis, multiplied efforts at certainty by said and aforesaids. (Tandon & Behn 5)

Technical Terms :-

Technical words are the words which are unfamiliar to a lay person. Most of the words in the legal discourse are technical and exclusive to the discourse of law and the range of legal words or the technical words is quite wide. Some of the legal words or the legalized words are- *Abate, Bail, Allege, Requisition, Domicile, Forfeit, Decree, Mortgage, Sub-letting, Deem, Permises, Tenant, Lease, Hereinafter, landlord,* and so on. Some of these are English words from common English Language, whereas many of them belong to the foreign origin.

Every field of study has its own characteristic vocabulary and so has the legal language. The terms like *Warranty, Deed, Criminal, Proceedings, Procurator Fiscal, Grantee, Devisee, Waiver, Furnish, and Covenant Demurrer* and so on are typically found in the legal language which makes it distinct. There are some other terms or words which have both the ordinary meaning and the legal meaning as well and obviously both differ. They are polysemic in nature and have high contextual meaning e.g. *Assignment, Maintenance, Consideration, Title.*

Archaic Expressions:-

Archaic expressions are the words, phrases, or grammatical structure that are no longer in usage. They are linguistic relics which are preserved in specific contents like literature, religious texts and in law. These expressions often come from Latin, Norman French, or Old or Middle English and persist largely due to legal traditions, precedents, the precision they lend to the legal documents and the formal tone they carry. In legal language the archaic expressions retain a powerful presence in certain fields where tradition, formality, and precision are highly valued through a gradual process of language formation. Legalese evolved as jargon language with such unique nature and nuances.

The word 'árchaic' has ancient roots and it comes from the French word 'archaique', which means ancient. The word's history reinforces its meaning that pertains to the beginning or ancient times. "Art of expression or efficiency in speaking is considered to be synonymous of the legal language." (Tripathi xxi)

Among the rarely used or archaic expressions are the adverbial expressions like *hereinafter, herein, hereto, hereby, hereof, whosoever, thereof, therein, heretofore, herewith, whereby,* and *wherefore*; said and such (as adjectives); verbs like to arraign (to clear a legal account or settle and accusation or controversy); nouns like surrejoinder (the answer by the plaintiff to a rejoinder by the defendant); adjectives like afore-said, and so on.

Deictic expressions in legal language refer to words or phrases whose meaning depends on the context in which they are used. Many deictic elements are adverbs, indicating time or place. They function as pointing words that refer to people (person deixis), places (place deixis) or times (time deixis) which makes legal drafting crucial. For example:-

-*As of now*, establishes a precise temporal starting point of the courtroom.

-The party hereby agrees, links the agreement directly to the person or entity uttering it.

The origin of such antiquated expressions can be traced back on Old English and, "may have originally been introduced as ambiguity resolving elements or means of abbreviation" (Hiltunen 84). These expressions make the legal documents more formal and distinct. Tiersma states that "legal language often strives toward great formality; it naturally gravitates towards archaic language". (95)

Jurists prefer to use the antique terms, 'inquire' in used in place of 'ask'; 'peruse' has been widely used instead of 'read'; 'forthwith' is a substitution of 'right away' or 'at once' or them. (Alcaraz & Brain 5). Moreover, the worlds like 'witnesseth' instead of simple 'witness' add an archaic flavor to the legal language.

Arbitrary Expressions :

Arbitrary expressions are often used in the legal language. The expressions 'of even date herewith' is used in place of the usual expression 'dated the same as this document'; 'these presents' instead of 'this document'; the date hereof instead of 'today'; 'in my said mother', instead of 'my mother; 'for the purpose of identification only more particularly delineated', instead of 'for identification only' or 'more particularly' delineated; 'jointly and severally' instead of 'separately and together'.

The use of such arbitrary expressions or the antiquated terminology adds complexity to the meaning and is advantageous also. Besides retaining the distinct identity of the legal language, it has other functions to perform as well. It helps to evade frivolous changes as the legal lexical meaning is taken into consideration. Crystal and Davy (213) rightly endorse it when they say that "what has been tested and found adequate is best not altered". The archaic and antiquated expressions have been tested and have received authoritative interpretation over the years. Moreover, the frequent use of rare Old English and Middle English gives archaic feel to legalese.

Words have different facets of meanings as per the context(s) and hence, sometimes it is considered better to retain the same archaic words. So the risk of finding difficulty in understanding is better than the danger of misinterpretation. Hence, the conservative legal terms are better often though they create barriers in the better understanding especially of the laypersons as they become more inaccessible to the common readers.

Latin and French Terms in Legal Language:

Anglo-Norman, a dialect of Old French played a crucial transitional role in the evolution of English legal language. Its legacy remains embedded in the terminology and tradition of the English legal system. It contributed to the development of legal bilingualism, where Latin was used for formal records, Anglo-Norman for oral proceedings, and later English for accessibility.

Legalese is highly influenced by Latin and French reflecting centuries of historical and institutional development. The continued used of these foreign terms serves an important function. The French and Latin terms provides precision, and convey a historical authority reflecting the deep roots of legal principles in Roman and Norman jurisprudence. The use of such terminology also contributes to the uniformity and consistency of legal interpretation across jurisdictions and over the time.

Since Anglo-Norman was the language of the courts, there were French borrowings into the legal English. Interestingly, Latin was used for the official documents. Due to the widespread opposition to the Latinized expressions, there was an unsuccessful attempt through the British Parliament in 1730 to abolish Latin expressions from the legal proceedings. However, Latin expressions had to be restored after short suspension. Blackstone (cited in Williams 65) has said that certain technical terms were "not capable of an English dress with any degree of seriousness". The only option was to retain those terms and are in usage since then. Legalese inevitably comprises of many Lain and French expressions (medieval and modern) in their original forms. In India we follow the British model of English and legalese is primarily English, therefore we find many French and Latin expressions in the legal discourse.

Many Latin terms are still in use which convey complex legal ideas with precision and authority. Terms like *'prima facie', 'pro bono', 'mens rea', actus reus', 'habeas corpus', 'de jure', and 'ex parte' are very borrowed from Latin whereas 'tort', 'a posteriori', 'verdict', 'parole', 'bailiff', 'alimony'* are borrowed from the French.

Many terms of Norman origin are still used in legal English e.g. *court, judge, appeal.* Some words are now not used in legal circles, e.g. *attainder* (the loss of civil rights through conviction of high treason). However such terms have become 'naturalized' as English words due to the consistent use of them in the usual functioning. A vast number of foreign lexical terms or expressions in legal texts originate from Latin, such as *ex parte* (on behalf of), *ratio legis* (the reason for, or principle behind, a law) etc.

Foreign expressions such as *Jurisdiction, alien, arbitrator, attorney, per capital, suo motu, statute, ex officio, ex parte, suo motu, inter alia* have assimilated in legal vocabulary in such a way that they are undistinguishable today from the other native expressions. However words like *mens rea, de facto, amicus curiae, prime facie, habeas corpus, corpus delicit, interalia,* though borrowed from foreign languages, have little place in today's normal English language, and are rarely used. The following list of Legal terms along with their meanings reflects upon the conventional usage and context where they are used.

- **sine die:** without arranging a date for another meeting
- **ad hoc:** for this purpose only
- **alias:** a name used other than the given name of a person
- **sub judice:** a legal case which is being considered by a judge or is an a court and some details of it cannot be discussed in public.
- **alimony:** support paid by one ex-spouse to the other as ordered by a court in a divorce case.
- **Bona fide:** evidence or proof that someone has sincere feelings or is who they claim to be Synonyms or related words for this sense of bona fides.
- **Res judicate:** an issue adjucated
- **De nova:** a new thing; an undecided question of law
- **Actus reus:** guilty act

Parsi -Arabic-Urdu Words:

In Indian legal language we find many Parasi-Arabic-Urdu words, which is the result of the 400 years of old Mughal Empire rule in India. The words like *Vakalatnama, Belif, hawaldar, mamletdar, kacheri, mofusil, talak, kabool, hokum* are still found in the legal language used in India in general and in Maharashtra in particular.

After the Norman Conquest in 1066, the language of the invaders gained an undeniable position in the legal sphere of England, bringing with it a wealth of legal French terminology (Crystal & Davy 208). Norman French became the language of law and the ruling class in England. Latin continued in the Church and Old

English remained the language of the common people. Thus, many new words were introduced in the legal language which influenced the development of Middle English and thus evolved a language from the blend of Anglo-Saxon and Norman influences. French remained the official language of the royal court and administration for centuries. Later as nationalism grew and English as a language became more established, the hold of French language diminished over time.

English is a borrowed language and so is law. The rulers affected the language and law equally. Hence, clear evolution through the impact of the invasions and emperors is apparent and evident in the legal language. The legal vocabulary contains many words of French origin viz. *appeal, bar, counsel, suit, estate, jury, lease, summon, tenant, verdict, contract, proposal, schedule, terms, conditions, policy, alias, quash* and so on. During the time of Christ, Latin became the language of law, court records and statues. However, it remained the language of the highly learned-class and could not become the legal language in strict sense as it was hardly used in pleadings and debates. Despite this, it left a mark on the legal language as the Latin terms like *ab intio, suo motu, ultra vires, bonafide, adhoc* got assimilated into the legal language. Such Latin terms and Latinized vocabulary has become the life and blood of legal language.

Chapter-6
The Language of the Law

Since time immemorial law and language have been associated with the human beings. Before the constitutional laws came into force, the God-given laws would be governed or the laws in the name of God were administered. Legal rights, duties, rules and regulations and obligations were incorporated in the form of contracts, wills, deeds, notices etc. Whether it was natural law or edicts of God or will of the sovereign or welfare law directing to serve justice and interest of society. Laws communicated through language have been the part and parcel of the society. Even in those days, laws were in force and so were language and the legal language. It is the elucidation and explication of laws through language that has make a difference. The aim has been the maintenance of a stable, peaceful and orderly society which has been enriched by laws ensured and interpreted through the lens of language. Both law and language have evolved gradually over a long period of time and have been amended considering the adaptability and the need of the society over the years.

It is quite interesting to note the origins of the words 'Law' and 'language' and find some commonalities between them. The word 'language' is derived from the Latin word 'lingua' that means *tongue*, whereas the word '*law*' is taken as an derivative of the verb 'leggja' which means laydown. Right from the Anglo-Saxon to the classical languages like Latin and Greek; from the old English and French to simple English of today, language as well as law has undergone significant changes. Adaptability and acceptability are key features of both law and language which is evident in the significant evolution of law and language, now the Law Speak.

There exists a very deep and subtle relationship between law and language. They are intertwined and weave together a scheme of words and phrases indispensable to the study of Law. Law is governed through language and is also governed by the grammatical rules of syntactic and lexicon patterns. Laws are coded in language and both inhabit every domain of our life. The legal fraternity uses language in order to articulate, discuss and implement laws.

Commenting upon the relationship between law and language, Prof. M.L A. Hart in *'Concept of Law'* opines that language has an 'open texture'. In *'Law Language and Communication',* Probert emphasizes 'word' consciousness' in law. Logical sense is equally important that way. Many legal terms are 'value impregnated' without serving any rational function as per *Glanville Williams.* Robert M. Dworkin views that "We are all beneficiaries or victims of what is done to the language we share". (Quoted, Tandon and Behl 02)

Law is fundamental to our life through language in the sembslance of rights, duties, wrongs, Acts of Parliament, Cases, Reports, documents like contracts, licenses, applications, forms, wills, agreements, transfers, notices, deeds; Court pleadings, summons, briefs, arguments, judgments; legal texts like books, journals, references, correspondence and so on. One has to be very cautious while using language in law as a slight misinterpretation may change the things considerably. Lord Mansfield has rightly said, *"Most of the disputes in the world arise from words.* "(Quoted, Tandon & Behl 2) Hence, proper study of grammar, punctuation, spelling, syntax, diction is quite necessary to say what is actually intended and desired, elusiveness, vagueness, ambiguity, lengthiness, verbosity and complexity are the defects in legal language arising out of the linguistic incompetence and stylistic imperfections. This shows the close or relatively inseparable relationship between law and language. Both are intertwined and interwoven in a fabric which is used in the legal discourse. Therefore legal language is imperative and in every form of legal writing, both legal and language skills play a significant role.

Though ignorance is bliss, ignorance of law is no excuse. It is rather contradictory. The knowledge of law is necessary and language should not be a barrier between the laws and the persons who want access to it. Law should be then comprehensible to all. In order to support this, the remarks of Peter Tiersma once quoted. He says:

"Legal language must be judged how clearly, concisely and comprehensively it communicates rights and obligations conferred by the Constitution, opinions expressed by courts, regulations embodied in statutes, promises exchanged in contracts. But unfortunately, a large chunk of legal text is shrouded in a dense, complex maze of archaic, verbose vocabulary." (Quoted, Tandon and Behl 10)

The language of law is unlike general English and it cannot be easily comprehended without the help of a legal expert. A lay man can be cheated and deceived on account of their ignorance of the laws and due to the incomprehensibility of the legal language. People face severe consequences due to lack of understanding of the legal terminology. In routine life while dealing with people in the banking sector, in matters related to insurance policies, share market, medical insurances, loans, deals and decrees people are usually deceived on account of their ignorance and inconsiderate approach. Thus, the knowledge of laws and rights has become more important today than ever before as it is directly connected to an individual's life and career. In today's era ruled by AI and Information and Technology there is a marked advancement in the way legal subjects are dealt with. Globalization, privatization, liberalization, the World Wide Web, smartphones, computers and other AI driven devices have brought many advances in the era of Information and Technology, questioning the interplay between the language and the application of language. However, along with these developments they have brought menaces as well. Smartphones are blissful. However, there is great negligence on the part of the users. It is a serious concern that many of us 'agree' to the terms and conditions laid down by the app providers least concerned about the content and give access to sensitive data which can breach our privacy. On various search engines like the Google apps we often give permissions and agree on multiple platforms and give access to our personal data on our Smartphones and other devices. Prior to agree, one must read the terms and conditions mentioned along with the legal clauses and consequences.

As discussed earlier, Legal language is the language used by persons related to the law field or legal profession. Traditionally English has been the language of lawyers from English-speaking countries viz. America, England, Canada, Australia, New Zealand, Kenya, and South Africa and so on. These countries have shared common law traditions. Owing to the colonial forces early on the trends of globalization, privatization and liberalization, import and export-international business, it has now become the language of the globe called as Lawspeak.

Hence, the language used by lawyers, judges, jurists, legislative draftsmen and other persons related to law fraternity is legal language. "Legal language is a varietal system of technical terms, situations meanings, complicated procedural arrangements etc which communicate at least among the law men in a unique style imperceptibly interwoven with certain juristic traits and judicial qualities." (N.R.Madhava Menon, quoted, Tandon & Behl 3)

Ashok Kelkar, a veteran law (legal) expert identifies five types of situational contexts wherein legal discourse or communication is evident (quoted, Tandon & Behl 4):

- The law giver to the judge and the counsel.
- The judge to the counsel and vice versa-judgments, briefs, courtroom exchanges and so on.
- Consultation among judges, counsels and men of law as part of legal discussions. This may be termed as informal as it takes place outside the court in the chambers of judges and advocates, offices of lawyers etc.
- Judge to the jury; counsel to the client and vice versa.
- Between ordinary citizens. This may include contracts, wills, agreements, bylaws, notices and other drafts.

The legal language or the legal English takes into its fold its use in the context of-

- legal documents: contracts, licences, etc.
- court pleadings: summonses, briefs, judgments, etc.
- laws: Acts of Parliament and subordinate legislation, case reports
- legal correspondence

National constitutions have come into existence by means of written language; laws and statutes are enacted, and contractual agreements between private individuals take effect.

There are different types of legal writing and all of them can be grouped together in the legal language. Though they differ marginally, the differences do exist. Goddard (2010) has discussed the following kinds of legal writing: (a) academic legal writing as in law journals, (b) judicial legal writing as in court judgments, and (c) legislative legal writing as in laws, regulations, contracts, and treaties. It is interesting to note that the legal English used in the academic writing which is reflected in the law journals, theses, dissertations, research papers and books is quite different from the

legal English found in the court judgments and in the laws and contracts. The purpose of writing and the intended readers determine the linguistic style of the legal writing. The academic touch and discursive note is quite evident in the journals and books. Legal English in the judgments differs primarily because the intended reader is usually a lawyer or lawyers who will in turn interpret the meaning to their clients. It is more authoritative and is more direct as well. The legal English found in the laws, contracts, treaties and agreements differs as it has the binding effect on the readers who could be the beneficiaries.

Apart from the above cited three types of the legal language(s), one more variety can be added which is the reader oriented legal language used by the lawyers in order to communicate with their respective clients especially when the lawyers are discussing a legal topic necessitated by their case (s). Hence, a legal expert or the person belonging to the law field communicating and interacting with a layperson uses legal language which is distinct from other three legal writing discourses. Hence, it is a variety within a variety; a register within a register. It is a legal discourse with more and more communicative competence and has more common words than found in the other three kinds of legal writing.

When two people not necessarily belonging to the legal field interact on a legal theme or topic, then also it would be termed as legal language. There would be minimum legal words and maximum everyday words. It is quite interesting and equally important to note that there is significant difference in the written legal language and the spoken legal language. Spoken language in legal discourse is equally essential as it comprises of the interrogation of plaintiffs and defendants in a courtroom, the testimony of witnesses, the pleadings by attorneys, their arguments, the cross examination, or the instructions from a judge to a jury.

A celebrated writer of the law discourse Urban Lavery (Edt. Bhatnagar) has argued that the lawyers are better speakers than writers. In his article entitled *The Language of the Law* he criticizes the lawyers for underprivileged writing. He has appreciated the lawyers' fluency and logic in spoken English and has highlighted many defects in their writing. It is a matter of great scrutiny whether to call those things as defects or characteristics. (33-34)

Legal language has its own characteristics. Some call them the properties and features and others call them defects. They are experts (especially the judges and lawyers) who feel that legal language as it is, is good and there is no necessity of making it plain, user-friendly, easily comprehensible to laypersons and so on. There are some linguists and veteran English professors who advocated continuation of the same legal language. For some the legalese is unique, distinctive and the legal fraternity uses it easily.

An honourable High Court Judge once said that the legal fraternity is used to the archaic words, intricate language, foreign words and phrases and so on. They feel quite comfortable using it. Hence, simplicity at the cost of beauty is unexpected and unnecessary. This reminds us of the poem *Pylons* where the poet speaks of the unearthed mountain. The mountain is beautiful in its entirety. When we dig it and try to see what is inside, it loses its beauty. So is the case with the legal language. If we focus more on communication part, the magnetism it has will get diminished.

A linguist and an author has approved of legal language as it is and opined that if one studies it minutely, it is not incomprehensible. According to him, closer look at the legal language does not make it remain beyond the reach of the laypersons. Moreover, to him, it is not possible to develop a register as per the requirements of individuals.

However, there are defenders of the plain language movement who are thinking of simplifying the legal language so that it will be within the reach and comprehension of the laypersons. Many linguists, authors, legal luminaries, teachers of law and many from legal fraternity have advocated the need of reader-friendly legalese. These experts have highlighted the defects in the legal language and have suggested measures, substitutes to the words and complicated expressions.Henceforth, if the principles of effective communication (the 7 C's) e.g. clarity, comprehensibility, courtesy, correctness, conciseness, completeness and consideration are strictly followed in the legal texts, the problem can be solved.

Will Rogers burlesques legal language by saying: "The minute you read something you can't understand, you can be almost sure it was drawn by a lawyer." (Quoted, Tandon and Behl 09) John Lindsay too satirizes the legal language while he says-

"Law books are the largest body of poorly written literature ever created by human race." (Quoted, Tandon and Behl 09) David Mellinkoff terms the legalese as *"wordy, pompous and dull"* whereas Lawrence Friedman opines that it is *"swaddled in obscurity."* Jeremy Bentham thought it to be "characterized by redundancy of language and unnecessary intricacies."(Quoted, Tandon and Behl 09)Annelize Nienaber has criticised it for its "obscure expression, Latin terms, technical jargon, wordiness, long complex sentences, seemingly meaningless repetitions and archaisms." (Quoted, Tandon and Behl 10)

Against this backdrop, it is imperative here to take note of both: the salient features and the so called defects in the legal language. An ornament for one may seem to be a defect to another. Tandon and Behl opines:

"No language is flawless, but legal language enjoys the doubtful distinction of being the most ridiculed language-its users are also its abusers." (9)

The opening lines of Prof. Fred Rodell's '*Goodbye to Law Reviews*' are: "There are two things wrong in almost all legal writings. One is style. The other is its content." (Quoted, Tandon & Behl 09)

Some of the main characteristics of written legal English are the sentence length and the complexity of its sentence structures, repetitiveness, the high concentration of Latinisms and archaic or rarely used lexical items etc. (Bhatia 77). Such features have been widely held for centuries as having an exclusionary function, entrenching the privileges of the legal profession. Reliance on authority and citation besides importance to precedent are other distinguishing features of the legalese. Legalese is often ambiguous, vague and loose in language and structure which allows various interpretations. The word 'right' means claim, exact, just, correct etc. depending upon the context. Hence, contextual meaning gains great importance. Ambiguous words are used in plenty. Verbosity is too frequently visible. The typical phrases and expressions like 'subject to', 'notwithstanding', 'provided' often peep into the legal texts. Here even the word legal has two meanings: legal versus illegal and legal versus general.

Logic and facts are the geneses of law. Legalese has been the language of ages known for its wisdom, reason, rationality and justice. Accuracy is the soul of it. Uniformity is its prime feature, though laws have been interpreted differently. From the time immemorial courts, judges and lawyers have been seen more respectable in the society as they are the last hope of the people. They are the last resort. Hence, besides doctors, advocates/lawyers have been held important in our society. Urban Lavery in his article entitled *The Language of the Law* speaks in the same tune:

"...the lawyer in his field-even as the physician and the priest in theirs-remains the last resource of other men and women. When the wisdom of common men fails them and disaster is at hand, when the layman's brain is overworked till his mental fuse burns out, when the motorcar of 'Business' blows out its tires and piles up in the ditches of insolvency, when the human derelict is finally tossed upon the rocks by the stormy seas of life, then the lawyer is sent for and his "quiddities" and his "quillets" are more than welcome." (Bhatnagar 33)

People have great faith in the judiciary and it is the only hope and last refuge when the world goes against them. It is the judicial system or the court where they trust and expect to have free, fair and impartial judgment. This belief, faith and trust is not gained in a day or year but has been the result of the experience of the centuries together. Even when the actual courts and lawyers were not in existence, the Caste and Community Courts called *Jaat Panchayat* played an important role and ensured justice. Presently in many communities and especially in the tribal communities, the Caste Courts have great importance. It's because these experts involved in conferring justice are having force and authority, the sanction and validation of many centuries and many civilizations. Hence, the lawyers and judges today are the part of that continuing tradition that has influences of Greeks, French, and Latin and so on. The contemporary laws and their administration is the unification of the complex web of various laws practiced in various countries that were dominating. The imperial influences are too obvious. The centers of world-wide authority changed over the stretch of time. As a result of this we had Greeks as superiors earlier followed by the Romans and the French and then the British and now the Americans leading the world in many walks of our life.

Altering with the legal language can be hazardous. The widely accepted and acknowledged meanings will be lost and there cannot be powerful and suitable equivalent to the legal words which are often termed as jargon, archaic and borrowed (foreign). Many words have a sort of force in them and the word is enough to convey the desired and expected meaning. Substitution of such words and expression may cause misinterpretation and subsequently miscommunication.

Legal language is not a distinct language as such. It is the contextual variety of any language. Legal language in general sense can be Marathi, Hindi, English or any language that has been used in the legal discourse or law fileds. However, if the world panorama is taken into consideration, English is used as the legal language all over the world. As legalese or legal language is not a separate or distinct language as such, the veteran linguist and Sahitya Akadami award winner Prof. Ganesh Devy claims that legal language is not a language but a register. It becomes imperative here to have a look at register and discuss how it is different from a language.

Oxford dictionary defines 'register' as a specialized variety of language used by legal professionals, characterized by specific technical vocabulary(legalese),complex syntax, archaic terms like 'hereof', 'null and void', all serving the specialized purpose of law in a particular social setting. Its focus is on the manner or way language is used in particular situations. It is further argued that "scholarly consensus has not been reached for the definitions of terms including 'register', 'field' or 'tenor'; different scholars' definitions of these terms are often in direct contradiction of each other. Additional terms including genre, text types, style, acrolect, mesolect and basilect, among many others, may be used to cover the same or similar ground. Some prefer to restrict the domain of the term 'register' to a specific vocabulary (Wardhaugh 1986) (which one might commonly call jargon), while others argue against the use of the term altogether." This argument takes to call legalese a genre. This will be supported by the, following explanation given in Wikipedia: "Genre is any category of literature, music or other forms of art or entertainment, whether written or spoken, audio or visual, based on some set of stylistic criteria." However, 'genre' does not appropriately fit to the legalese socialistically due its characteristic features. It can be, to some extent, termed as the textual type as it is at times descriptive, narrative, expository, and argumentative. Legalese can be distinguished from its counterparts from its stylistic features as well.

Legalese can well said to be a jargon also. As mentioned and discussed in previous chapters also, it is imperative here to define jargon. "Jargon is a type of language that is used in a particular context and may not be well understood outside of it." It is further explained that "The context is usually a particular occupation, like a certain trade, profession, or academic field, but any in-group can have jargon. The main trait that distinguishes jargon from the rest of a language is special vocabulary—including some words specific to it and, often, narrower senses of words that out-groups would tend to take in a broader sense." (Wikipedia)

Oates & Enquist have distinguished between the legalese and the legal language i.e. legal English (English used in the law discourse) (127). They consider it to be a pejorative term associated with a traditional style of legal writing. It belongs to the special discourse of the lawyers which "lay readers cannot readily comprehend". Hence, the legalese is the typical language which is supposedly beyond the reach of the lay persons. It has its own characteristics and like the classical languages Latin, it appears rich but is beyond the reach of billions of readers and users. When Oates & Enquist term it as pejorative, they are necessarily talking about the poor legal writing which is "cluttered, wordy, indirect, and uses unnecessary technical words or phrases". (Butler 32.) Such salient features have kept the legalese boundless to the lawyers. Every language has the basic communicative purpose but the legalese seems to have it restricted to the law fraternity. It is completely different from the ordinary discourse. Hence, the language used in the legal drafting of the contracts and statutes or in the pleading differs significantly from the everyday use of English. This gives special importance to the lawyers because of which they have occupied a specialized position in the society. This is true in the context of the religious scriptures and treatises as well. The common people always relied on the secondary sources as the primary sources were incomprehensible to them. Hence, the word of the god did not directly reach out to the masses. The masses had to and have to depend upon the interpretation of the 'religious agents' for the meanings from the religious texts. The reader-unfriendly issues of the legalese have been taken up by the activists of the Plain Language Movement. The promoters and supporters of plain language argue that legal "writing style should not vary from task to task or audience to audience...; whatever lawyers write must be clear, correct, concise, and complete". (Wydick 3) However, it must be agreed and accepted that there is bound to be difference and distinction between different discourses wherein the language is determined by the context-formal vs. informal and so on. Hence, though it is a valid argument to expect the legalese to be clear, correct, concise and complete, one has to accept that the complexity and wordiness are determined by the discourse which is often inevitable. Besides the four Cs proposed by the proponents of the plain language, some other Cs are imperative in effective communication viz. comprehensibility, considerateness, courtesy. When these Cs are added to the previous four Cs, legalese will be communicative. Wydick says that these Cs are the "characteristics of good legal writing style" in the United States.

English is undeniably an international language today. Due to its global presence in almost all regimes, it has become more important today than ever before. It was the British influence in India that introduced English language to the Indians who were colonized and were expected to be better workers for facilitating administrative purposes. However, today English has become the part and parcel of Indian life. It will not be exaggeration to say that English is called the life-line today as abridge language. It has surpassed Hindi and has become a sort of national language linking and bringing together people belonging to different and diversified cultures, geographical regions, mindsets, attitudes and so on. It will not be an exaggeration to term it as a language that has united people under an aegis. English in India has been the language of trade and commerce and with globalization at its height, import and export is as common as the use of English for its purpose. It is the library language and the language of education.

There is a significant paradigm shift in the realm of English Language Teaching (henceforth ELT) in India. The communicative approach has been followed everywhere so that the students become conversant in English after their schooling. The use extensive use of ICT in education has changed the educational scenario significantly. The gap between the literate and the illiterate, between the educated and the uneducated is narrowing. The rural and tribal area are also witnessing sea change with the students from such neglected areas coming out with flying colours. Mobile phones and computers, ipads with AI driven devices have become very common today. The introduction of MALL and CALL in the teaching of English and the concepts like edutainment and infotainment has become catch-phrases. English is seen being used in all the sectors from education to entertainment and from fashion to fantasy. Many literary artists have proved their mettle producing masterpieces and many of them have been acknowledged world-wide and few of them have received prestigious awards.

Chapter-7
Legal Terms and Legal Maxims

Legal maxims have been an integral part of the legalese. Their foreign origin often complicates the discourse and their manifestation makes the language rich and sophisticated. Legal maxims, derived largely from Roman jurisprudence, function as concise doctrinal suggestions that illuminate the underlying logic of legal systems across jurisdictions. Although not binding rules of law in themselves, these aphoristic expressions possess persuasive authority, guiding courts in interpreting statutes, resolving ambiguities, filling doctrinal gaps, and articulating principles of equity, fairness, and natural justice. Their enduring relevance lies in their ability to distill complex legal concepts into universally comprehensible propositions—such as the insistence on culpable intent in '*actus non facit reum nisi mens sit rea*', or the demand for procedural fairness in '*audi alteram partem*'. Yet, legal maxims are neither absolute nor mechanically applied, rather they operate contextually, requiring judicial discretion to balance their historical origins with contemporary legal realities. In this way, maxims serve not merely as linguistic relics, but as dynamic interpretive tools that maintain coherence and continuity in the evolving fabric of modern jurisprudence.Legal maxims serve several dynamic functions within the structure of modern jurisprudence. They operate as interpretive aids that help courts clarify legislative intent, resolve statutory ambiguities, and articulate principles where written law is silent or insufficient. Maxims also reinforce consistency by anchoring judicial reasoning in long-established doctrinal foundations, thereby promoting coherence and predictability in legal outcomes. In areas such as equity, natural justice, and procedural fairness, these maxims provide normative guidance that shapes judicial discretion and safeguards fundamental rights. Furthermore, by condensing complex legal ideas into concise expressions, they facilitate legal education and intellectual clarity, enabling lawyers, judges, and scholars to grasp foundational principles quickly. Thus, legal maxims function not merely as rhetorical devices, but as essential tools that support interpretation, coherence, fairness, and continuity across legal systems.

Legal maxims are established principles or propositions of law expressed in Latin. Courts often rely on these maxims while interpreting statutes, determining rights, and resolving ambiguities. Below is a consolidated list of major legal maxims frequently used in Indian and common-law jurisprudence, along with leading case laws.

Audi Alteram Partem

Meaning: No one should be condemned unheard.

Principle: Every party must be given a fair opportunity to present their case.

Case Laws

- Maneka Gandhi v. Union of India (1978): Passport impounded without giving reasons; court held that fair hearing is essential.
- Ridge v. Baldwin (1964): Dismissal without hearing held void.

Nemo Judex in Causa Sua

Meaning: No one should be a judge in his own cause.

Principle: Bias vitiates judicial and administrative decisions.

Case Laws:

A.K. Kraipak v. Union of India (1969): Rule against bias applied in administrative actions.

Dimes v. Grand Junction Canal (1852): Judge disqualified due to pecuniary interest.

Actus Non Facit Reum Nisi Mens Sit Rea

Meaning: An act does not make a person guilty unless the mind is also guilty.

Principle: Criminal liability requires both actus reus and mens rea.

Case Laws:

- State of Maharashtra v. Mayer Hans George (1965): Explained the role of mens rea in statutory offences.
- R v. Prince (1875): Classic distinction between strict and mens rea offences.

Ignorantia Juris Non Excusat

Meaning: Ignorance of the law is no excuse.

Principle: A person cannot escape liability by claiming lack of knowledge of the law.

Case Laws:

- State of Maharashtra v. M.H. George (1965): Ignorance of foreign exchange regulations not accepted.
- Hira H. Advani v. State of Maharashtra (1971).

Ignorantia Facti Excusat

Meaning: Ignorance of fact is an excuse.

Principle: Honest mistake of fact can be a defence.

Case Laws:

- R v. Tolson (1889): Mistaken belief of husband's death was valid defence.
- Keso Sahu v. State of Bihar (2000).

Res Ipsa Loquitur

Meaning: The thing speaks for itself.

Principle: In negligence cases, circumstances may imply negligence without direct proof.

Case Laws:

- Scott v. London & St. Katherine Docks (1865).
- Municipal Corporation of Delhi v. Subhagwanti (1966).

Res Judicata

Meaning: A matter once decided is decided forever.

Principle: Prevents re-litigation of the same issue between the same parties.

Case Laws:

- Satyadhyan Ghosal v. Deorajin Debi (1960).
- Daryao v. State of U.P. (1962).

Stare Decisis

Meaning: To stand by what is decided.

Principle: Courts should follow previous judicial decisions for consistency.

Case Laws:

- Bengal Immunity Co. v. State of Bihar (1955): Discussed departure from precedent.
- Keshav Mills Co. Ltd. v. CIT (1965).

Ubi Jus Ibi Remedium

Meaning: Where there is a right, there is a remedy.

Principle: Violation of a legal right must have a legal remedy.

Case Laws:

- Ashby v. White (1703): Violation of voting right led to remedy.
- Bhim Singh v. State of J&K (1985): Illegal detention; compensation awarded.

Volenti Non Fit Injuria

Meaning: No injury is done to a person who consents.

Principle: Consent is a defence in tort law.

Case Laws:

- Hall v. Brooklands Auto Racing Club (1933): Spectator assumed risk.
- Padmavati v. Dugganaika (1975).

Caveat Emptor

Meaning: Let the buyer beware.

Principle: Buyer must check quality and suitability of goods.

Case Laws:

- Ward v. Hobbs (1878).
- Bhagwati Prasad v. Union of India (1962).

The lexicon of English legal words, terms and expression is not exhaustive but nevertheless sufficient for the beginner law inquisitors.

Accused	The person charged. The person who has allegedly committed the offence.
Acquittal	Discharge of defendant following verdict or direction of not guilty.
Act	Law, as an act of Parliament or Legislature.
Action	It has same meaning as the word *CLAIM.*
Adjourned generally or *sine die*	Temporary suspension of the hearing of a case by order of the Court (maybe for a short period, *e.g.,* to next day or *sine die).*
Adjournment	The postponing of the hearing of a case until a later date.
Adjudication	A judgment or decision of a court, tribunal or adjudicator in alternative dispute resolution (ADR) cases where disputes are resolved outside of the court.
Administrative Court	The Administrative Court is part of the High Court. It deals with applications for judicial review.
Administration order	An order by a County Court directing a debtor to pay a specified monthly installment into Court in respect of outstanding debts. The Court retains the payments made and at

	intervals distributes it between the creditors on a *pro-rata* basis.
Admiralty	An admiralty claim is a claim for the arrest of a ship at sea to satisfy a debt.
Admission (including part admissions)	A party involved in a claim may admit the truth of all or part of the other party's case, at any stage during proceedings. For example, a defendant may agree that he or she owes some money, but less than the amount being claimed. If the defendant makes an admission, the claimant may apply for judgment, on the admission. See Section 17 of the Indian Evidence Act which states that admission is a statement of facts.
Adoption	An act by which the rights and duties of the natural parents of a child are extinguished and equivalent rights and duties become vested in the adopter or adopters, to whom the child then stands in all respects as if born to them in marriage.
Adultery	Voluntary sexual intercourse between a married person and another person who is not the spouse, while the marriage is still valid. This is a common fact relied on for divorce.
Advocate	A barrister or solicitor or a Lawyer representing a party in a hearing before a Court.
Adversarial	Arrangements designed to bring out the truth of a matter, through adversarial (conflict based) techniques such as cross-examination.
Affidavit	A written statement of evidence confirmed on oath or by affirmation to be true and taken

	before someone who has authority to administer it.
Affirmation	Declaration by a witness who has no religious belief, or has religious beliefs that prevent him/her taking the oath. They declare by affirmation that the evidence he/she is giving is the truth.
Alternative dispute resolution	These are schemes such as arbitration and mediation which are designed to allow parties to find a resolution to their problem, without legal action. A party's refusal to consider ADR could lead to sanctions (penalties) against that party, by a Judge, even if the party wins the case.
Amendment	The process by which corrections to court documents, such as statements of case, can be made. A statement of case can be amended at any time, before it is served or with permission of all other parties or the court, (once served). The court may reject the amendment, even if the party concerned has permission of other parties to the case.
Appeal	Application to a higher court or other body for review of a decision taken by a lower court or tribunal. The higher court may overturn or uphold *(i.e.,* reject) the lower court's decision. Often, permission (leave) is required, to for an appeal to occur.
Appellant	A person appealing to a higher court or body against a decision made in a lower court or body.
Applicant	Person making the request or demand, *e.g.,* person who issues an application.

Application	The act of applying to a civil court to ask it to do something, for example to start proceedings.
Appraisement or appraisal	Valuation of goods seized under warrant of execution prior to sale.
Arbitrator or Arbitration	A process in which both sides agree to use an independent arbitrator (an impartial person) who gives a binding decision in the matter. The person making the claim (claimant) has to choose between going to arbitration and court-it is not usually possible to take a claim to court after it has been through arbitration
Bail	Release of a defendant from custody, until his/her next appearance in Court, subject sometimes to security being given and /or compliance with certain conditions.
Bailiff	Bailiffs and enforcement officers are people authorised to remove and sell possessions in order to pay the money a debtor owes to a person or an organisation. They may also conduct evictions, and arrest people. A bailiff can also serve (deliver) court documents on people.
Bankrupt	Insolvent-unable to pay creditors and having all goods/ effects administered by a liquidator or trustee and sold for the benefit of those creditors; as a result of an order under the Insolvency Law.
Bar	The collective term for barristers or Advocates or Lawyers or Solicitors.
Barrister	*Counsel. A* member of the Bar: a lawyer or an Advocate entitled to represent clients in all the

	courts. There is a historical difference between Barrister and Advocate/Lawyer/Pleader/Vakil.
Bench warrant	A warrant issued by the judge for an absent defendant to be arrested and brought before a Court.
Bill of indictment (U.K.)	A written statement of the charges against a defendant sent for trial to the Crown Court, and signed by an officer of the Court.
Bind over (U.K.)	In the Crown Court or (more usually) the Magistrates Court, and signed by an officer of the Court.
Bind over for sentence	An order which requires the defendant to return to Court on an unspecified date for sentence. Failure to observe this order may result in a forfeiture or penalty to be enforced.
Bound/binding	A binding decision is one that must be obeyed by the people concerned. For example, it is not possible to go to court after a binding decision has been issued by an arbitrator.
Brief	Written instructions to counsel to appear at a hearing on behalf of a party prepared by the solicitor and setting out the facts of the case and any case law relied upon.
Case	An action, suit or claim in a court of law. It can also mean the arguments put forward by parties in a court of law.
Case disposal	The case is taken out of the court process.
Case Management	This is a meeting between all parties to a case and the Judge to check the progress of the case, with regards to costs and other matters.

Conference (CMC)	The numbers of CMCs held depend on the complexity of the case.
Case management tracks	Civil cases are allocated to one of three case management tracks, depending on financial value, issues of law and the likely duration (length) of the case. The three tracks are (i) the small claims track in which cases to the value of five thousand pounds can be considered and the claimant does not have to have legal representation (ii) the fast track for cases of value between five and fifteen thousand pounds and (iii) the multi-track for cases of value over fifteen thousand pounds. Legal representation is advisable in the fast and multi-tracks.
Case number	A unique reference number allocated to each case by the issuing Court.
Case value	The financial value of a case - known as case value - is one of the factors used to assess which track a case (claim) should be allocated to. *See* also case management tracks above.
Caution	(i) Notice given to the Land Registry by any person with an interest in particular land to ensure that no action is taken in respect of the land without the person's knowledge. (ii) Warning, given by a Police Officer, to a person charged with an offence. (iii) Warning, given by a Police Officer, instead of charge.
Caveat	A notice given to the registrar that effectively prevents action by another party without first notifying the party entering the caveat.

Cessate	A grant of representation of limited duration which has ceased and expired.
Chambers	(i) Private room, or Court from which the public are excluded in which a District Judge or Judge may conduct certain sorts of hearings (ii) Offices used by a barrister or Advocate or Lawyer.
Chancery Division	The Chancery Division is part of the *High Court* in U.K. It deals with cases involving land law, trusts and company law.
Charge	A formal accusation against a person that a criminal offence has been committed *(see Criminal Procedure Code, 1973)*
Charging Order	A court order directing that a charge be put on the judgment debtors' property, such as a house or piece of land to secure payment of money due. This prevents the debtor from selling the property or land - without paying what is owed to the claimant.
Circuit Judge	A Judge between the level of a High Court Judge and a District Judge, who sits in the County Court and/or Crown Court (U.K.).
Civil	Matters concerning private rights and not offences against the State.
Civil case or claim	A civil dispute that involves court action. *See* also the word claim or action.
Civil Justice or civil law	A branch of the law which applies to the rights and dealings of private citizens, (including such matters as unpaid debts, negligence and the enforcement of contracts).

	It does not include criminal, immigration, employment or family matters.
Claim	Proceedings issued in the County or High Court. Previously know as an Action. *See* also civil case or civil claim.
Claimant	The person issuing the claim. Previously known as the Plaintiff.
Claim form	Proceedings in a civil court start with the issuing of a claim form. The form, which is issued by the court (after the claimant has filed the form in court), includes a summary of the nature of the claim and the remedy (compensation or amends) sought.
Codicil	An addendum signed and executed which amends or adds something to a Will.
Coercion	Coercion exists when an individual is forced to behave in a particular way, by threats of violence, for example. The person concerned does not act freely.
Collaboration/ collaborative	Working together to solve a problem.
Commercial Court	Part of the Queen's Bench Division of the High Court.
Commissioner of Oaths Committal	Solicitors authorised by the Lord Chancellor to administer oaths and affirmations to a statement of evidence (i) Committal for trial: Following examination by the Magistrates of a case involving and indictable or either way offence, the procedure of directing the case to the Court to be dealt with

	(ii) Committal for Sentence: Where the Magistrates consider that the offence justifies a sentence greater than they are empowered to impose they may commit the defendant to the Court for sentence to be passed by a Judge (iii) Committal Order: An order of the Court committing someone to prison (iv) Committal Warrant or *WARRANT OF COMMITTAL.*
Common Law	The law established, by precedent, from judicial decisions and established within a community, a single system of law worked out by legal experts, the common law, the law common to all England.
Compensation	Usually a sum of money offered in recompense (to make amends) for an act, error or omission that harmed someone. The harm suffered may have been loss, personal injury or inconvenience.
Complainant	A person who makes a complaint.
Complaint	Expressing discontent for something.
Concurrent Sentence	A direction by a Court that a number of sentences of imprisonment should run at the same time.
Concurrent Writ	A duplicate of the original writ bearing the same date and expiring at the same time as the original.
Conditional Discharge	A discharge of a convicted defendant without sentence on condition that he/she does not re-offend within a specified period of time.

Conduct Money	(i) Money paid to a witness in advance of the hearing of a case as compensation for time spent attending Court. (ii) Commonly used to describe expenses paid to a debtor to cover the costs of traveling to Court.
Consecutive Sentence	An order for a subsequent sentence of imprisonment to commence as soon as a previous sentence expires. Can apply to more than two sentences.
Contempt of Court	Disobedience or wilful disregard to the judicial process. In civil cases, for example, failing to appear as a witness without informing the court or the party that called you. A person found to be in civil contempt of court could be fined.
Contents of trial (civil)	Trial contents.
Contributory Negligence	Partial responsibility of a claimant for the injury in respect of which he/she claims damages.
Co-respondent	A person named as an adulterer (or third person) in a petition for divorce.
Corroboration	Evidence by one person confirming that of another or supporting evidence, for example forensic evidence (bloodstain, fibres etc.) in murder cases.
Costs (civil) and Compensatory Costs	In civil proceedings the general rule is the person who wins the case is entitled to his or her costs. The court may decide to reduce the costs to be paid by the losing side if it feels that the winner has behaved unreasonably.

	The award of costs is at the court's discretion. *See* sections 35 and 35A Civil Procedure Code.
Counsel	A Barrister or solicitor in legal proceedings.
Count	An individual offence set out in an indictment.
Counterclaim	A claim made by a defendant against a claimant in an action. There is no limit imposed on a counterclaim, but a fee is payable according to the amount counterclaimed.
Court of Protection	The branch of the High Court with jurisdiction over the estates of people mentally incapable of handling their own financial affairs.
Court fees	The Court will charge to issue a claim in a civil case and to launch enforcement proceedings if the defendant ignores the judgment of the court. You will also be charged if you make applications to the court.
Courtroom	The room in which cases are heard.
Court sanction	Penalty imposed by court.
Covenant	A formal agreement or a contract constituting an obligation to perform an act.
Creditor	A person to whom money is owed by a debtor.
Criminal	Person who has been found guilty of a criminal offence.

Cross-examination	The questioning of a witness for the other side in a case.
Damages	An amount of money claimed as compensation for physical/material loss, *e.g.*, personal injury, breach of contract.
Debtor	A person who owes money to someone or to an organisation.
Decree	An order of the Court in proceedings commenced by petition.
Decree Absolute	A final certificate, resulting from an application, dissolving a marriage.
Decree Nisi	Order for divorce unless cause to contrary is shown within a set period.
Declaration	Court order setting out the rights of a party in the form of a statement.
Deed	A legal document which sets out the terms of an agreement, which is signed by both parties.
Defence or defending a claim (civil)	When the defendant disputes the claim made by the claimant.
Defendant (civil)	The person who has a claim made against them. They can defend (dispute the claim) or admit liability, in part or in full.
Defendant (criminal)	Person standing trial or appearing for sentence.
Disability	The inability of a person to handle their own affairs *(e.g.,* through mental illness or a minor under 18 years of age) which prevents

	involvement in civil legal proceedings without representation.
Disclosure	Parties to a civil case must disclose (show to the other party) documents they intend to rely on in court to support their case.
Discovery of documents	*INSPECTION OF DOCUMENTS;* Mutual exchange of evidence and all relevant information held by each party relating to the case.
Discontinuance	Notice given by the Court, on instruction by the claimant that they no longer wish to proceed with the case.
Dismissal	To make order or decision that a claim be ceased.
Disposal	Case disposal either by court process or out of court process.
Dispute	A civil problem not dealt with in court, (a civil dispute which comes to court is called a civil case); challenging the views of the opposing party in a civil case
District Judge	A judicial officer of the Court whose duties involve hearing applications made within proceedings and final hearings subject to any limit of jurisdiction Previously known as Registrars.
Divisional Court	As well as having an original jurisdiction of their own, all three divisions of the High Court have appellate jurisdiction to hear appeals from lower Courts and tribunals. The Divisional Court of the Chancery Division deals with appeals in bankruptcy matters from the County Court. The Divisional Court of the

	Queen's Bench Division deals largely with certain appeals on points of law from many Courts. The Divisional Court of the Family Division deals largely with appeals from Magistrates Courts in matrimonial matters a 'next friend' or 'guardian *ad litem'*.
Divorce	Dissolution or nullity of marriage.
Dock	Enclosure in criminal Court for the defendant on trial.
Either-way Offence	*Indictable Offence, Summary Offence:* An offence for which the accused may elect the case to be dealt with either summarily by the magistrates or by committal to the Court to be tried by jury.
Enforcement	Method of pursuing a civil action after judgment has been made in favour of a party. Process carried out by Magistrates Court to collect fines and other monetary orders made in the Crown Court.
Entry of Judgment	Decision of the Court in favour of one or other of the parties.
Estate	The rights and assets of a person in property.
Evidence	Documentary or other material which is used to support a person's case in a court of law.
Execution	Seizure of debtor's goods following nonpayment of a Court order. Execution of decree I a civil suit.
Executor	A person or persons specified to carry out the provisions of a will.
Exempt	To be freed from liability or allegiance.

Exhibit	Item or document referred to in an affidavit or used as evidence during a Court trial or hearing.
Expert Witness	Person employed to give evidence on a subject in which they are qualified or have expertise.
Filing	The process of delivering or presenting forms and other documents to a court. For example a claim or a defense to a claim must be filed.
Guarantor	Someone who promises to make payment for another if payment is not made by the person responsible for making the repayments of a loan or hire purchase agreement.
Guardian	A person appointed to safeguard/protect/manage the interests of a child or person under mental disability *(Next Friend)*
Hearing	A hearing is the trial of the case. Hearings are usually held in public.
High Court	A civil Court which consists of three divisions:— (i) Queen's Bench (can be known as King's Bench Division if a King is assuming the throne) - civil disputes for recovery of money, including breach of contract, personal injuries, libel /slander; (ii) Family - concerned with matrimonial maters and proceedings relating to children, *e.g.,* wardship; (iii) Chancery - property matters including fraud and bankruptcy

	High Court as per the Constitution of India Articles 214-231.
Indictable Offence	A criminal offence triable only by the Court. The classification of different types of offences.
Infant	Also known as a minor: A person under 18 years of age which prevents them from acting on their own behalf in legal proceedings (To be represented by parents or guardians or next friend).
Injunction	A court order which either restrains a person from a course of action or behavior, or which requires a person to follow another course of action.
Insolvency	*Bankrupt.*
Inspection of Documents	*Disclosure of documents:* Arrangements made by the parties to allow mutual exchange and copying of documents.
Instalments	A method of paying a debt in several parts at intervals. Payment by instalments is agreed to make the burden of repayment lighter.
Interest	A charge for borrowed money, a percentage of the sum borrowed.
Interlocutory	Interim, pending a full order/decision, *e.g.,* interlocutory judgment for damages pending further hearing to assess amount to be awarded and entered as final judgment.
Interpleader	A claim by a third party to ownership of goods levied upon under a warrant of execution which is disputed by a creditor. The Court then issues an interpleader summons for

	the parties to attend Court to adjudicate on rightful ownership
Intestate	Without leaving a Will.
Interim order	An order made during proceedings which is not a final order.
Issue/issuing	To initiate legal proceedings in pursuit of a claim.
Judge	An officer appointed to administer the law and who has authority to hear and try cases in a court of law.
Judgement	The decision or sentence issued by a court in legal proceedings.
Judgement set aside	A judgment or order can be set aside (made void) at the request of a party to the case in certain circumstances, for example if they were too ill to attend court on the day of the judgment
Judicial review	The Higher Judiciary (Supreme Court and/or High Court) can review decisions of inferior (lower) courts, public bodies and other regulatory bodies to ensure that the decision making process has been lawful.
Junior Counsel	*(Counsel) A* member of the bar: the branch of the legal profession which has rights of audience before all Courts.
Jurisdiction	The area and matters over which a court has legal authority.
Juror	(see *Jury) A* person who has been summoned by a Court to be a member of the jury (Not applicable in India).

Jury	Body of jurors sworn to reach a verdict according to the evidence in a Court (Not applicable in India).
Jurisdiction	The area and matters over which a Court has legal authority.
Juvenile	Person under 17 years of age.
Landlord	A person or organisation which owns land and/or buildings which are leased to tenants.
Landlord and Tenant Act	Act which empowers applications (seeking extension of a lease or some other action concerning tenancy.
Law	The system made up of rules established by an act of parliament, custom or practice enjoining or prohibiting certain action.
Lawyer	The legal profession in the UK is divided into two branches. Barristers have the right to represent clients in higher courts whereas most solicitors are restricted to represent their clients in the lower courts .In India, under the Indian Advocates Act, 1961 there is only one class of legal professionals, that is, Advocate.
Lease	The letting of land or tenements, *e.g.,* rent etc., for property for a prescribed period.
Leave	Leave means 'permission'. Some steps in legal action require the permission of the court. For example a losing party may be granted leave to appeal.
Legal advice	Advice about the law and your options from a qualified legal representative or advice centre.

Legal Aid/Public Funding	State funded assistance, for those on low incomes, to cover legal fees. Legal Services Authority Act in India enjoins the provisions for Legal Aid process.
Legatee	Person to whom personal estate is given by Will.
Letters of Administration	Authority granted by a Probate Registry to someone interested in the estate of a person who has died without' leaving a will. The order allows the 'administrator' to carry out the duties relating to the estate.
Levy	A duty carried out by a bailiff or sheriff under the authority of a warrant or writ *oifi-fa,* for a sum of money whereby goods of value belonging to the debtor are claimed with a view to removal and sale at a public auction in an attempt to obtain payment.
Liability	Responsibility or obligation. For example, a debt is a liability or responsibility.
Libel	A written and published statement/article which infers damaging remarks on a person's reputation.
Licence	Permission to carry out an act that would otherwise be considered illegal.
Lien	A legal right to withhold the goods/property of another until payment is made.
Litigation	Legal proceedings or court action. Litigation can be either civil or criminal proceedings.
Magistrates Court	A Court where criminal proceedings are commenced before justices of the peace who examine the evidence/ statements and either

	deal with the case themselves or commit to the Court for trial or sentence. Also has jurisdiction in a range of civil matters. Chief Judicial Magistrate.
Maintenance Pending Suit	A temporary order for financial provision made within divorce proceedings until such time as the proceedings are finalized *(i.e.,* by issue of the Decree Absolute),
Mal-administration	Mal-administration is administration that leads to injustice because of such factors as excessive delay, bias or arbitrary decision-making.
Master	*(Registrar)* Judicial officer of the High Court in the Royal Courts of Justice who normally deals with preliminary matters before trial.
Master of the Rolls	Senior Judge of the Court of Appeal (Civil Division).
Matter	*(Originating Application)* Proceedings commenced by way of originating application.
Mediation	A process for resolving disagreements in which an impartial third party (the mediator) helps people in dispute to find a mutually acceptable resolution. If mediation fails court proceedings can be initiated or re-activated.
Minor	Someone below 18 years of age and unable to sue or be sued without representation, other than for wages. A minor sues by a next friend and defends by a guardian.
Mitigation	Reasons submitted on behalf of a guilty party in order to excuse or partly excuse the offence

	committed in an attempt to minimize the sentence.
Mortgage	A loan of money advanced to purchase property. The transfer of the property is withheld as security for payment.
Mortgagor	The party obtaining the loan.
Mortgagee	The party that advances the loan.
Motion	An application by one party to the High Court for an order in their favour.
Notary Public	Someone who is authorised to swear oaths and certify the execution of deeds. *See* also Oath Commissioner.
Nullity	Application to the Court for a declaration that a marriage be declared 'void' or be annulled *i.e.,* declared never to have existed or to have subsisted until the Court dissolved it.
Oath	To call upon God to witness that what you say at the hearing is the truth or binding, *(affirmation).*
Objection	Disagreement within argument or set out by another at the hearing.
Ombudsman	Independent 'referees' who consider complaints against public and private organisations in a wide range of fields including housing, health and banking. They are often used as a last resort when complaints cannot be resolved through an organisation's own complaints procedure. Ombudsman services are free to use. Recommendations made by ombudsmen are not binding on the person making the complaint (complainant).

	They can still go to court even if the ombudsman decided against them.
Order	A direction by a Court.
Particulars of claim	This document contains details of the claimant's claim which must be contained in the claim form or served shortly after the claim form has been served. The particulars should be a concise statement of the facts of the claim.
Party/parties	People involved in court proceedings either as the defendant(s) or claimant(s).
Petitioner	A person who presents the petition,
Plaintiff	*CLAIMANT* in civil suits.
Plea	A defendant's reply to a charge put to him by a court; *i.e.,* guilty or not guilty.
Pleading	Documents setting out claim/defence of parties involved in civil proceedings.
Possession Proceedings	Legal proceedings by a landlord to recover land or property such as a house or flat.
Precedent	The decision of a case which established principles of law that act as an authority for future cases of a similar nature.
Probate	The legal recognition of the validity of a will.
Process	The document commencing a claim or subsequent action.
Prosecution	The institution or conduct of criminal proceedings against a person.
Prosecutor	Person who prosecutes *(PROSECUTION)*.

Quash	To annul; *i.e.,* to declare no longer valid.
Quasi-judicial functions	A quasi-judicial function is an executive function that involves the exercise of discretion (judgment). Court staff perform quasi-judicial executive functions such as managing the issuing of claims, serving court documents and deciding what would be reasonable for the defendant to pay - for example, see determination.
Quantum	In a damages claim the amount to be determined by the court.
Respondent (Civil & Crime)	The defending party (person) in an appeal or in a petition to the courts. Also Appellant.
Restitution	Where a defendant who has been evicted by a bailiff illegally re-enters the property the claimant must issue a warrant of restitution with the court in order to regain possession.
Settlement	A voluntarily agreement by the claimant and defendant to settle their civil case.
Sheriff	An officer of the Crown whose duties, amongst other things, consist of the enforcement of High Court writs of execution. In India Sheriff of Mumbai who performs similar functions for Government and Judiciary.
Solicitor	Member of the legal profession chiefly concerned with advising clients and preparing their cases and representing them in some Courts. May also act as advocates before certain Courts or tribunals. Solicitor General of India.

Subpoena	A summons issued to a person directing his/her attendance in Court to give evidence.
Suit	Legal proceedings commenced by petition.
Suitor	Person bringing a suit before the Courts.
Summons	Order to appear or to produce evidence to a court.
Surety	A person's undertaking to be liable for another's default or non-attendance at Court.
Tenant	A person which holds land or property under a lease.
Testator	A person who makes a Will.
Third party	Person who is not party to a legal case, but may be relevant because he or she owes the defendant money. In that case the defendant can issue a third party notice against such a party.
Tort	An action in tort is a claim for damages to compensate the claimant for harm suffered. Such claims arise from cases of personal injury, breach of contract and damage to personal reputation. As well as damages, remedies include an injunction to prevent harm occurring again.
Trial	A public hearing in which the evidence in a case, and the law which applies, are examined.
Trial (civil)	Civil trials are generally held before one or more judges without a jury. The form and length of a civil trial will depend on the track to which the case has been allocated

Tribunal	A tribunal is a body outside of the court structure. They hear disputes relating to specific areas such as immigration, employment and some tax matters and adjudicate on them. Tribunals are thought to be cheap and fast and allow expert knowledge to be applied.
Trust	Property legally entrusted to a person with instructions to use it for another person (or persons benefit).
Trustee	A person who holds or administers property in a trust for another (or others).
Undertaking	A promise, which can be enforced by law, made by a party (person) or their legal representative during legal proceedings.
Verdict	The finding of guilty or not guilty by a court.
Voluntary	Something is voluntary when it is entered into without compulsion, as a result of the free choice of the person(s) concerned.
Will	A declaration of a person's intentions to distribute his/her estate and assets.
Winding up	The voluntary or compulsory closure of a company and the subsequent realisation of assets and payment to creditors.
Witness	A person who gives evidence in Court, called to give evidence because they witnesses an event (Also *Expert witness).*

Chapter-8
Legal Language as English for Specific Purposes (ESP)

English for Specific Purposes (ESP) is a subset of applied linguistics that focuses on teaching and analysing language used in specific domains such as medicine, engineering business, and law. In the sphere of teaching ESP includes Business English, Technical English, Scientific English and Legal English more specifically called Legalese or Law Speak. The term ESP refers to the language of research and teaching that focuses on the specific communicative needs and practices of particular social groups. It is focussed on the language suitable to need-based activities in terms of grammar, lexis, study skills and discourse. Legal English stands out as a particularly complex and formalized variant of English that serves the needs of the legal profession across jurisdiction. It is characterised by a specialized vocabulary, distinct grammatical structures and a formal register. Evans Dudley has discussed the 'absolute' and variable characteristics of ESP.

Absolute Characteristics:-

- ESP is defined to meet specific needs of the learners.
- ESP makes use of the underlying methodology and activities of the discipline it serves.
- ESP is centred on the language appropriate to a particular activity in terms of grammar, lexis, etc.
- ESP utilizes methodologies pertinent to the disciplines it serves.

Variable Characteristics:-

- ESP may be related to or designed for specific disciplines.
- ESP may use a different methodology from that of general English.
- ESP is likely to be designed for learners at tertiary level in the educational institutions.
- ESP is generally designed for intermediate or advanced students.

Ramachandra Ashok Kelkar, a veteran legal expert and linguist identifies five types of situational contexts wherein legal discourse or communication is evident. In these legal contexts communication is structured and formal, which demands linguistic precision and perfection.

- The judge to the counsel and vice versa in judgements, case briefs and courtroom exchanges.
- Consultation among judges and counsels and men of law.
- Judge to the jury and counsel to the clients and vice versa.
- Between ordinary citizens- includes wills, contracts, agreements, drafts etc.
- Amongst the legal fraternity for communication.

The Legal Texts can be classified in two ways, Informative and Normative. Informative Legal Texts merely gives information and normative legal texts plays an important function which is prescriptive, wherein a course of action has been mentioned. The principal function of these texts is to keep the human relations in order which determines its general illocutionary force, which aims to impose obligations, give permission and confer rights. Sarcevic, as a researcher discussed the normative nature of legal language and legal texts in relation to legal translation. Sarc opines that "Normative texts prescribe how the member of a given society should act (command), refrain from acting (prohibition), may act (permission) or are explicitly authorised to act (authorisation)". The Normative texts are formal, written in high impersonal style which according to Williams "helps to reinforce the idea of impartiality and authoritativeness''. This includes texts like Constitutions, Statutes, Ministerial orders, Contracts, Wills, Deeds and judicial and international treaties and conventions. Legal texts are not homogeneous, they serve multiple purposes and communicate different types of information. One of the most foundational distinctions in legal writing and legal interpretation is between normative and informative texts. Understanding this distinction is essential for legal analysis, legislative drafting, and judicial interpretation.

The characteristics, functions, and interactions of normative and informative elements in legal discourse demonstrates how normative texts establish legal norms. While informative texts assist in explaining, interpreting, and applying these norms. Both are indispensable to the functioning of legal systems.

Normative Legal Texts:

The Normative Legal Texts are the ones that, that recommends and endorse the Law. Normative legal texts are those that prescribe the conduct and behaviour. They establish legal obligations, rights, permissions, and prohibitions. These texts create binding rules that must be followed by individuals, organizations, and institutions. Such texts are typically found in:

- Constitutions
- Statutes and codes
- Regulations

- Contracts and treaties
- Judicial orders

The Linguistic Features of these Normative texts includes Normative language which is characterized by its prescriptive modality. Common modal verbs and expressions include:

- shall, must, may not, is prohibited from, has the right to, is obliged to

These verbs signal the presence of legal norms. For example:

- "The defendant shall appear before the court within 30 days."
- "No person shall be deprived of liberty without due process of law."

The key feature of normative texts is their binding legal force. These texts have a normative force. Breaching a normative rule typically results in legal consequences such as fines, penalties, or invalidation of actions. For example, failing to comply with a statutory deadline may result in the dismissal of a legal claim.

Informative Legal Texts Explaining the Law Informative legal texts do not prescribe behavior directly. Instead, they explain, clarify, or interpret legal norms. Their primary function is to provide context, resolve ambiguity, and support reasoning in legal decision-making. These texts can be found in:

- Judicial reasoning and opinions
- Legal commentaries and treatises
- Explanatory memoranda attached to laws
- Law textbooks
- Legislative history documents

Linguistic Features

Informative texts are descriptive or analytical rather than prescriptive. They use language that defines, explains, and reasons. Examples include:

- means, refers to, includes, is interpreted as, according to, it is generally understood that

Example:

- "In this context, 'public authority' refers to any governmental body authorized to act under national law."

Role in Legal Interpretation

Informative texts play a crucial role in statutory interpretation, constitutional analysis, and contractual construction. They help judges and lawyers understand the intent behind a legal norm or how it has been interpreted in prior cases. For example, a court might refer to legislative history or a legal commentary to clarify ambiguous statutory language.

There is an Interplay between Normative and Informative Texts. Legal documents often contain both normative and informative elements. A single statute may contain binding rules (normative) alongside definitions or legislative intent explanations (informative).Judicial Decisions frequently blend the two. The holding or order is normative (e.g., "The appeal is dismissed.")The reasoning is informative, offering analysis and interpretation. This combination allows courts to apply legal norms while also developing legal doctrine through explanatory discourse. In Legislative drafting, the influence of the normative and informative is clearly visible. The Legislative bodies may attach explanatory notes to bills. While these notes are not legally binding, they provide essential context and can be referenced in court to interpret the law's purpose. Example:

- Normative section: "Any person who engages in fraudulent trade practices commits an offense."
- Informative note: "This clause is intended to capture digital and traditional forms of deceptive commercial conduct."

These texts are of immense importance in Legal Education and Practice

Understanding the distinction between normative and informative texts is vital for the Law students, who must learn to identify binding rules vs. background explanation. It is imperative for the Judges and lawyers, who use informative texts to interpret norms and construct arguments. The Legislators, who aim for clarity and precision in drafting laws.

The inability to distinguish between the two can lead to misinterpretation, such as treating a non-binding commentary as law or ignoring informative context when applying a rule. Example: Free Speech in Constitutional Law

Consider the following constitutional provision as for example.

- "Every individual has the right to freedom of expression." (normative)

A court case interpreting this provision may involve:

- Reference to prior decisions defining "expression" (informative)
- A discussion of limitations such as hate speech laws (normative + informative)
- Examination of the framers' intent from constitutional debates (informative)

The court's final decision on whether a specific law violates freedom of expression is normative, but its justification is built upon layers of informative material. The legal system depends on both normative and informative texts. Normative texts create the structure of law by prescribing duties, rights, and prohibitions. Informative texts enrich the legal landscape by offering clarity, context, and interpretive guidance. Both types are essential for a functioning legal system that is both rule-bound and reasoned. For students, scholars, and practitioners, the ability to recognize and navigate between these two forms is crucial for effective legal reasoning, argumentation, and communication. A deeper understanding and more persuasive legal practice.

Chapter-9
Scope and Domain of Legal Language

Language is the foundation of communication in every human society, but in specialized domains, language takes on unique characteristics to serve specific purposes. One such domain is the legal system, where precision, clarity, and consistency are paramount. Legal language also referred to as 'legalese' is a specialized form of communication used in all forms of communication in laws, statutes, regulations, contracts, and judicial decisions. Its main function is to express legal norms, obligations, rights, and procedures with minimal ambiguity. Legal language or legalese is not merely ordinary language applied in legal contexts it constitutes a distinct register, already discussed in the previous chapters, with its own syntax, vocabulary, stylistic features, and communicative purposes. It operates at the intersection of law and language, reflecting both the technical requirements of the legal system and the social values it seeks to protect.

Scope of Legal Language

The scope of legal language refers to its range of usage and the extensiveness of contexts in which it functions. Legal language is multi-faceted and encompasses the following areas:

- ***As Legislative and Statutory Language:***

Legal language forms the backbone of legislation. Statutes, ordinances, and regulations rely on precise constructions to define rights, duties, prohibitions, and penalties. The scope here includes drafting laws and regulations, codifying norms systematically, and ensuring alignment with constitutional and international provisions.

- ***As Judicial Language:***

Courts utilize legal language in judgments, legal opinions, arguments, and court orders. Clear articulation ensures accurate interpretation of statutes and precedent, maintaining judicial consistency and fairness.

- ***As Contractual and Commercial Language:***

Legal language is used in contracts, agreements, and commercial documents to define obligations, avoid disputes, and anticipate contingencies. The precise construction of rights and duties minimizes litigation risks.

- ***Administrative and Procedural Language:***

Administrative bodies bank on legal language for notices, licenses, internal regulations, and regulatory frameworks. Clear and concrete language ensures compliance and facilitates enforcement.

- ***International and Comparative Law:***

Legal language extends to treaties, conventions, and international agreements, ensuring diplomatic clarity and harmonization of norms across jurisdictions.

Domain of Legal Language:

The domain of legal language refers to the conceptual and functional boundaries within which it operates. It is shaped by the unique requirements of the legal system which is predominantly observed with the following features in multifarious domains.

- ***Precision and Formality:***

Legal language prioritizes exactness over stylistic elegance. Words are selected for unambiguous meaning, technical specificity, and legal enforceability.

- ***Stability and Conservatism:***

Legal language tends to be conservative, preserving historical continuity and preventing unintended changes in legal interpretation.

- ***Interpretative Nature:***

While striving for clarity, legal language often requires interpretation due to vagueness, evolving societal contexts, and judicial discretion.

- ***Technical Vocabulary:***

Specialized terms such as *'tort', 'mens rea'* and *'prima facie'* convey specific legal concepts and facilitate consistent understanding among legal professionals.

Legal language is evolving in response to global changes and technological advancements. Integrating technology along with Ai assisted legal drafting is the most important challenge to be faced in the times to come. The future envisions a code-based legal language, which might use blockchain as used in crypto currency. The Gen Z, Gen Alpha and Gen Beta would be experiencing an entirely new domain of hybrid legal language which could be a blend of law + programmed legal language of coding. Efforts would be made to standardise legal terminology across multiple spheres leading to a multilingual legal communication globally. In near future legalese would become less ceremonial, more precise, technologically enhanced and human –centered without losing legal force.

Works Cited and Consulted List

- Alabi, Victoria A. *Stylistic Features of the Legal Discourse/* www.ajol.info/index.php/ujah/article/viewFile/102581/92850
- Amsterdam/Philadelphia: John Benjamins.
- Anbhule, Rahendra. Constitutional Law of India, Pune: Hind Law House. 2010.
- Bentham, Jeremy. The Works of Jeremy Bentham. Edited John Bowring. Edinburgh: W. Tait, 1843..
- Bhatia V. K. Analyzing Genre. Language Use in Professional Settings. London: Longman, 1993.
- Bhatnagar, R.P., Law and Language. New Delhi: Macmillan India Ltd, 2004.
- Bhuvan's Scientific Investigation of Death Cases, Prayag Publishing Company, Allahabad, 2008.
- Bowers, Frederick. Linguistic Aspects of Legislative Expression. Vancouver: University of British Columbia Press, 1989.
- Chomsky, N. Language and Mind, New York: Harcourt Brace Jovanovich, Inc.. 1968.
- Denning, Lord. The Discipline o f Law. London: Butterworth's, 1979.
- Garner, Bryan. Legal Writing in Plain English. Chicago Press, 2013.

- Givón T. 1993. English Grammar. A Function-based Introduction, vol. 1.
- Gotti M. Specialized Discourse. Frankfurt: Peter Lang, 2003.
- Gustafsson, Marita. Some Syntactic Properties of English Law Language. University of Turke: Publications of the Department of English, 1975.
- Hale, Mathew. A History of Common Law in English. Harvard: Harvard University Press. 1971.
- Halliday, M. A. K. Introduction to Functional Grammar. London: Edward Arnold, 1985.
- Hiltunen, Risto. The Types and Structures of Clausal Embedding in Legal English. Helsinki: Suomalainen Tiedeakatemia, 1984.
- J&K State Land Grants Act, 1960.
- Jackson, B. S. Making Sense in Law. Liverpool: Deborah Charles Publications, 1995.
- Legal Information Institute, Cornell University Law School. Retrieved 14 August 2016.
- Longman. Dictionary of Language Teaching and Applied Linguistics. London/New York: Longman, 2002.
- Maley, Yon. The Language of the Law. In John Gibbons (ed). Language and the Law. London: Longmans, 1994.
- Matthews, P.H. The Concise Oxford Dictionary of Linguistics, Oxford: Oxford University Press, 1997.
- Merriam Webster Dictionary. Available from Internet: <http://www.merriam-webster.com/dictionary

- New Oxford American Dictionary. 2nd edition. Oxford: OUP, 2005.
- Oates, L. & Enquist, A. Just writing: Grammar, Punctuation, and Style for the Legal Writer (Rev. ed.). New York: Aspen Publishers, 2009.
- Retawade, R.S. Legal Drafting, Pune: Hind Law House, 2014.
- Šarcevic S. New Approaches to Legal Translation. The Hague: Kluwer Law
- International, 2000.
- Schane, Sanford. Language and the Law. London: Continuum, 2006.
- South Australia Vs Peat Marwick Mitchell & Co. Supreme Court of South Australia Olsson J, 15 May 1997.)
- Swift. Jonathan. Gulliver's Travels. Oxford: Basil Blackwell, 1959.
- Thompson, Devy. Reading and Discrimination. London: Chatto and Windus, 1996.
- Tripathi, S.C. Legal Language. Legal Writing and General English. Allahabad: Central Law Publications, 2004.
- United State v. Wilson, 503 U.S. 1992. www.advocatekhoj.com. Accessed 18.2.17
- Williams, C. Legal English and Plain Language: An Introduction. ESP Across Cultures, 2004.
- Wydick, Richard C. Plain English for Lawyers, Carolina Academic Press, 1994.
- www.reference.com accessed 11.12.2016

- www.wikipedia.com accessed 17.11.2016
- www.univsource.com/words/circumlocution-noun.htm accessed 1.12.2016
- www.advocatekhoj.com accessed 10.10.2016
- www.univsource.com/words/circumlocution-noun.htm accessed 22.10.2016